Architectural Design
January/February 2007

Elegance

Guest-edited by
Ali Rahim + Hina Jamelle

WILEY-ACADEMY

ISBN-13 9780470029688
ISBN-10 0470029684
Profile No 185
Vol 77 No 1

Editorial Offices
International House
Ealing Broadway Centre
London W5 5DB

T: +44 (0)20 8326 3800
F: +44 (0)20 8326 3801
E: architecturaldesign@wiley.co.uk

Editor
Helen Castle

Production Controller
Jenna Brown

Project Management
Caroline Ellerby

Design and Prepress
Artmedia Press, London

Printed in Italy by Conti Tipocolor

Advertisement Sales
Faith Pidduck/Wayne Frost
T +44 (0)1243 770254
E fpidduck@wiley.co.uk

Editorial Board
Will Alsop, Denise Bratton, Mark Burry, André
Chaszar, Nigel Coates, Peter Cook, Teddy Cruz,
Max Fordham, Massimiliano Fuksas, Edwin
Heathcote, Michael Hensel, Anthony Hunt,
Charles Jencks, Jan Kaplicky, Robert Maxwell,
Jayne Merkel, Michael Rotondi, Leon van
Schaik, Neil Spiller, Ken Yeang

Contributing Editors
Jeremy Melvin
Jayne Merkel

Front cover: Contemporary Architecture Practice,
Commercial Office Tower, Dubai, United Arab
Emirates, 2005–. Facade detail. © Ali Rahim and
Hina Jamelle/Contemporary Architecture
Practice

Requests to the Publisher should be addressed to:
Permissions Department,
John Wiley & Sons Ltd,
The Atrium
Southern Gate
Chichester,
West Sussex PO19 8SQ
England

F: +44 (0)1243 770571
E: permreq@wiley.co.uk

Subscription Offices UK
John Wiley & Sons Ltd
Journals Administration Department
1 Oldlands Way, Bognor Regis
West Sussex, PO22 9SA
T: +44 (0)1243 843272
F: +44 (0)1243 843232
E: cs-journals@wiley.co.uk

[ISSN: 0003-8504]

D is published bimonthly and is available to
purchase on both a subscription basis and as
individual volumes at the following prices.

Single Issues
Single issues UK: £22.99
Single issues outside UK: US$45.00
Details of postage and packing charges
available on request.

Annual Subscription Rates 2007
Institutional Rate
Print only or Online only: UK£175/US$315
Combined Print and Online: UK£193/US$347
Personal Rate
Print only: UK£110/US$170
Student Rate
Print only: UK£70/US$110
Prices are for six issues and include postage
and handling charges. Periodicals postage paid
at Jamaica, NY 11431. Air freight and mailing in
the USA by Publications Expediting Services
Inc, 200 Meacham Avenue, Elmont, NY 11003
Individual rate subscriptions must be paid by
personal cheque or credit card. Individual rate
subscriptions may not be resold or used as
library copies.

All prices are subject to change
without notice.

Postmaster
Send address changes to 3 Publications
Expediting Services, 200 Meacham Avenue,
Elmont, NY 11003

CONTENTS

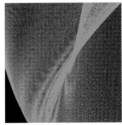

Editorial

Elegance exudes cultural self-confidence. It directly brings to mind the timeless splendour of a Palladian villa or the dignified presence of a London Georgian town house. It evokes the sophistication and allure of early 20th-century Parisian *haute couture* and the stylish lines of a classic car. For the first 50 years, architecture has not even raised its head above the parapet and aspired to be visually pleasing or graceful. It has been about everything but elegance. It has been technologically innovative, clever, rational, symbolic, sustainable, contextual, ironic, gritty and even downright ugly or brutal.

When Ali Rahim and Hina Jamelle of Contemporary Architecture Practice approached me and proposed 'elegance' as a theme for an issue, the idea sung out in its immediacy. Rahim and Jamelle are using it as a term to define a distinct body of work by some of the world's leading architects: Asymptote, Mark Goulthorpe of dECOi, Zaha Hadid Architects, Greg Lynn FORM and UNStudio. These are all designers who even a decade ago were regarded as avant-garde as much for their innovative digital techniques as for their experimental designs. They were so much to the side of the main field that they appeared to have little hope of getting anything sizable built.

No less progressive today, they can now be considered arbiters of taste. This is demonstrated by Hadid's recent completion of the Phaeno Science Centre in Wolfsburg, Germany, and UNStudio's Mercedez-Benz Museum, Stuttgart – the Phaeno Science Centre being the centrepiece of a redevelopment plan that puts Wolfsburg on the map, and Mercedez-Benz epitomising a top brand's alignment with a cutting-edge architectural form. This type of work is creating excitement and confidence among clients and the general public. Both these buildings have been widely featured across Europe on TV and in the national presses. Both the attention that current architecture gains from the world at large and architects' self-assurance in their own design skills has lifted the bar both in terms of technical and aesthetic ambition. It seems indicative of a new era of self-possession. Architects no longer feel the need to apologise through their muted or inverted expressions for their perceived Modernist misdemeanours. Elegance is architecture at the top of its game, reasserting architecture's position as a primary art. ∆

Helen Castle

This photograph, taken by Henri Cartier-Bresson in 1946 of Jeanne Toussaint, the designer and director of Cartier, is composed to explicitly express the elegance of the sitter. Note not only Toussaint's angled pose, but also the backdrop of silk drapes and upholstery.

Elegance in the Age of Digital Technique

Ali Rahim and **Hina Jamelle** of Contemporary Architecture Practice introduce this issue of *AD* by exploring how elegance represents a maturity in digital design practice. In order to undertake this new level of formal sophistication, mastery of technique and innate creative ability have to be combined with a multilayered design complexity. It is only then that the architect is able to fully tackle the multiple constraints and external demands of a project in gestation.

Greg Lynn FORM, Alessi Flatware, Venice, California, US, 2006
A family of elegant features and forms constitute mutations between each piece of tableware.

Why Elegance?

Beyond the austerities of digital techniques, elegance concerns refinement, precision and formal opulence. It integrates an aesthetic desire, unleashing a visual intelligence pertinent for all design fields at all scales. The concept of elegance has the ability to push forward the discourse of contemporary architecture by accepting that complex architectural compositions require an accompanying visual aesthetic as sophisticated as the current techniques used to generate form.

Elegance mediates and enables complexity. A tightly controlled, precise refinement in technique is required to mould transformative surfaces that incorporate distinctly different topological features. The results are potentially chaotic. Negotiating and restraining the visual opulence of these compositions is an operation that requires elegance.

The works and works-in-progress presented in this issue probe the concept of elegance, displaying a simultaneous maturation of digital and material practice. But beyond this refined mastery of technique, the architects move towards an integration of an aesthetic desire that yields elegant results.

Digital Tools, Elegant Forms

Elegance that has arisen from the use of relational equations and scripting mediated by digital techniques includes subdivision surfaces and NURBS modelling, tools that incorporate the most advanced results of experimentation in digital design. Progressive digital techniques are pivotal to moving forward in the field of architecture. But the design research, mastery of techniques and sheer talent required to produce the most sophisticated contemporary projects enabled by digital techniques are often taken for granted.

Elegance confronts this shortcoming in critical discourse by arguing that the mastery of technique, whether in design, production or both, does not necessarily yield great architecture. Even the most advanced techniques can still yield average, or even terrible, designs, and only certain projects that are sophisticated at the level of technique achieve elegance. This issue of *AD* highlights some of the instances in which designers have moved beyond techniques, by mastering them to such a degree that they are able to realise nuances that exude elegance within the formal development of their projects.

Architects who have been able to add this layer of aesthetic sophistication to their designs share several characteristics. All of the designers featured operate within emerging paradigms of generative techniques and have moved past methods completely dependent on the rigorous application of scientific standards. Each exhibits a systemic logic of thought that eschews mapping a specific process or revealing the process of an algorithm being generated as strategies to generate a project's form. Instead, mastery of technique allows them to assume a more sophisticated relation to the creation of form – a position made possible only through the use of an aesthetic sensibility concomitant with a highly developed design ability.

Design ability enables such architects to incorporate the myriad conditions for architectural creation including, though not limited to, constraints associated with zoning, building codes, organisation, space, programme, circulation, fabrication, assembly and cost, in a process facilitated by the digital algorithm and enabled by scripting. In the most elegant of designs, scripting is used to develop new types of interrelational schemes that integrate all design and manufacturing intentions in one seamless model. Ultimately, the architect's challenge is to control the modulation of these relations, in order to endow each project with the desired affects.[1]

The Pursuit of Elegance
Creating elegance in architecture can begin with the use and mastery of the digital techniques offered by customisable software. A reliance on scripting procedures rarely yields an elegant project, but manipulation of code through the mediation of digital techniques is essential to yielding elegance. Working through the process of mastering techniques is internally driven, and a necessary underpinning to developing a sensibility for the formal features realised through the course of design.

Frei Otto used one parameter to generate all of his landmark research on tensile structures – that of gravity's relationship to the coefficient of material elasticity. Driven by an interest in the minimal use of materials, his research employed analogue computing methods to yield results whereby singular features – for example, a catatonic curve or a derived surface – repeated themselves to produce larger formal organisations. However, these analogue methods did not have the capacity to produce two competing relational criteria as a means of generating form.

As architecture's multiple complexities are difficult to condense into a single formal criterion, it becomes apparent that a more interrelational set of criteria is needed to develop architecture through emergent methods. As more parameters are incorporated, the ability for a greater number of formal features to emerge becomes possible. The presence of several relational criteria allows for a family of interrelated features and forms to be included in the work. However, these arise only with specific intentions or goals for a project. When multiple criteria are employed, the formal design development is subsumed within the techniques used – the final design does not necessarily reveal the process of its creation. Hence, the process of production cannot be conceptually read in the final form that results from the design act.

The act of design is, therefore, ultimately framed not by a singular aesthetic end, but by the multiple constraints and ambitions of each project, as negotiated by the architect. To develop elegant work, layered levels of design intelligence are required, effortlessly incorporating organisational and spatial aspects.

Organisationally, the traditional concept of programme is redefined through the visible relationships produced by precisely controlled use-potential. In this definition, use-potential may yield relationships that emerge through the ongoing interactions between the user and the spaces. Spatial configuration and organisation act as criteria relational to the form of the project. The interior reveals its internal organisation through the gradually transforming relationships it forms to the human body moving through the space. In addition, this internal organisation is adapted to site constraints and the environment it operates within. Elegance is achieved when, rather than allowing external constraints to alter and compromise the internal organisation, the internal organisation is manipulated and transformed to adapt to external constraints. Again this requires a developed design and aesthetic sensibility, as reliance on technique alone yields average buildings.

Once repertoire and technique are controlled through coordination, formal features allow for gracefulness and movement, revealing the precision and mastery that can be accomplished with specific techniques. Through its graceful aspect, the external appearance of the form allows the internal organisation and its sophistication, experienced in movement through the space, to be perceived. The seamless transformation between internal and external organisation puts the internal techniques and their mastery on display externally.

Elegant structures possess formal features and material articulation that are rich enough to emphasise the realm of bodily sensation. This is also developed through the techniques and procedures used in the design. Buildings that

Melike Altinisik, Samer Chamoun and Daniel Widrig, Patrik Schumacher/Yusuke Obuchi Studio (Architectural Association DRL), New urban lobby addition, Centrepoint, London, 2006
The precision of transformation between the existing structure and the new building is key to the development of elegance. As the tower transforms from the surface of the building, it accumulates intelligence as it moves from a linear extrusion of a vertical structure to a pocketed project that distributes load differentially. As the mutation occurs, the interior relationships of inhabitation also change. This is evident in the transformation of the pockets of space that are contiguous to discrete spaces contained by the accumulation of material as they become spaces that perform as ramps.

Peter Mitterer and Matthias Moroder, Zaha Hadid Studio (Universität für Angewandte Kunst, Vienna), Mixed-use Tower, Istanbul, Turkey, 2006
The landscape contains features that respond to the scale of the site. Vehicular access with park-like functions is incorporated into the tower's base. As the surface turns up from the surface of the landscape into the tower, the features are mutated and do not repeat. Different rhythms are achieved by two rates of change adjacent to one another and driven by internal organisational issues – high-speed elevators that connect at the global scale of the tower, and a series of stairs that connect more locally. These adjacent rhythms are hybridised to produce a range of formal features in the tower. The continuity of surface transformation and modulation assists in the creation of elegance.

Janice Tan, Hina Jamelle Studio (Pratt Institute Graduate School of Architecture), Mixed-use tower, Battery Park City, New York, 2006
A family of features develops on the facade of the building producing different affects that conflate with its internal organisation to produce different organisations of work space. In essence this shifts environments on the interior as they respond to different porosities in the surface of the facade that allow different levels of light to penetrate into the interior. Integral to the project's elegance is the mutation of the facade into different internal features such as pockets and continuous surfaces.

can produce elegant sensations have particular formal characteristics, such as presence, formal balance, refinement of features and surface, and restrained opulence.

An elegant building needs to have a framework against which its presence is read and, at the same time, must participate as an extension of the field in which it operates. And formal balance results when the refinement of transformational spatial configurations creates forms that seemingly defy gravity. An exceptionally sophisticated integration of structure, systems and new materials may allow for the form to appear suspended, or possessed of a particular lightness. In terms of formal appearance, this lightness includes qualities of fineness and daintiness, determined within the multiple individual elements that constitute the building design. The scale of the part to the whole needs to be attenuated, and adjusted with precision and refinement, to produce the desired affects. If the scale of the part is too diminutive in relation to the whole, or if the whole has too many smaller pieces, then the viewer may be overwhelmed and the potential of producing elegance is lost. When the relation of part to whole is attuned, elegant sensations – rather than chaotic ones – may be achieved at the point of transformation.

To produce elegant sensations, the architect must design the project with the intention of elaborating refined surfaces to develop transformations between different formal features. The formal opulence of a building is realised through the creation of a family of formal features that are distinctive, yet remain interrelated as they transform from one to another. In an elegant composition, each feature is endowed with differences, and the transformation between features is attenuated and gradual. Transformations between features are mediated by a surface modulated in accordance with the transformation. These areas of change are constructed as deviations from a rule-generated surface, embedding geometrical characteristics within the perceptual and material circumstances of building. The surface itself is key, as it provides a background for the features to be made legible, ultimately providing the perspective necessary for the features to yield affects.

The Presence – and Future – of Elegance

Relational equations and scripting mediated by digital techniques are powerful allies in producing, manufacturing and assembling architectural projects that yield elegant sensations. An increasingly prevalent trend is the development of digital models that, in addition to incorporating formal constraints, integrate aspects of material and cost in one seamless model. Here, design intelligence moves beyond effective use of the CNC mill or laser cutter towards a highly integrated model that can compute costs dependent on factors such as material curvature and joinery. The customisation of these parts and their modulation, fabrication and assembly provides a bespoke quality to the architecture. Thus, the formal attributes of architecture developed during the design process may integrate nuances of negotiation with fabrication industries, directly reducing the cost of mass customisation.

The pursuit of elegance, here, incorporates a wider range of technologies in its quest to create elegant aesthetics manifest in built architecture. Mastery of technique remains important and underpins the use of digital technologies in the design and manufacturing of elegant buildings. But ultimately it is a highly sophisticated formal language – including the driving force of aesthetic pleasure – that propels elegance. ⚐

Note
1. 'Affects' are used throughout this article in plural to differentiate from 'effect'. Affects are defined as the capacity both to affect and be affected, whereas effect implies a one-way direction of causality. We are interested not in linear and predetermined types of effect, but in affects – unintended outcomes that have the power to create new results and causes. For a more detailed explanation see Ali Rahim, *Catalytic Formations, Architecture and Digital Design*, Routledge (New York), 2006, pp 136–9.

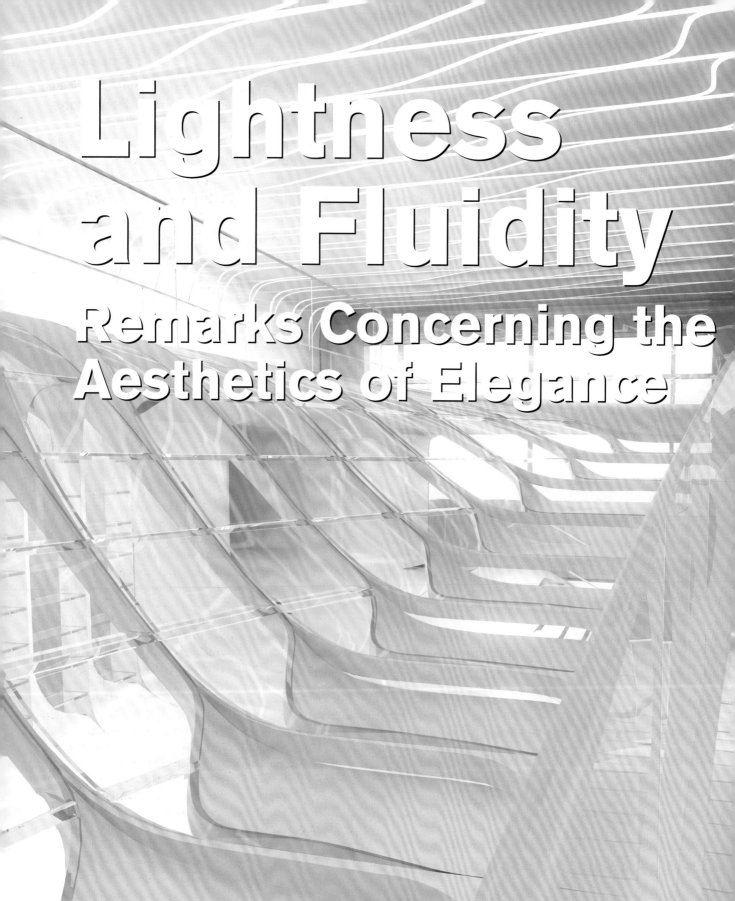

Lightness and Fluidity

Remarks **Concerning the** Aesthetics of Elegance

Over the last century, elegance as a term has been conspicuously absent from discussions centred on both architecture and the philosophy of aesthetics. Elegance's time has, however, now come. **David Goldblatt** describes how the maturation of digital discourse has led to the onset of a new, multifaceted, sensual rationality that is evident in recent designs and constructed works.

In recent years, self-conscious, digitally employed techniques in architectural practice have helped to spur to prominence an aesthetic dimension for architecture and have re-returned it to a sensuality undervalued in Modernist and Postmodernist building. Associated with the sensual, elegance is an elusive and compound aesthetic quality supervenient upon other properties – aesthetic as well as nonaesthetic. Its prominent features may change as context changes, so that what is characteristic of elegance in one work may be irrelevant to elegance in another. It is noteworthy that elegance, while used often and with abandon in many popular arenas, has been largely absent from the discourse of philosophy and architecture.

Aspects of a new elegance, some might say, save the architectural skin from unattended mechanism, mere formalism, extreme functionalism and theoretical indifference. However, a response to surface alone is not the story here. The departure from a pure formalism is achieved as traces of process are internally embodied as elegant qualities in architectural formations. Elegance leads architecture once again to emphasise a sensuous role for a mediating machine. With a nod towards the subjective, accidental and anthropomorphic, an architecture embedded with digital techniques has helped to create a greater balance between physiology and rationality, the cognitive and the affective.

Elegance incorporates a diverse set of contemporary architectural projects, some contributing to art history still merely as exciting potential. For example, Zaha Hadid's celebrated computer imagery as well as her built works such as the Leipzig BMW Motorcar Company and Wolfsburg Phaeno Science Centre are elegant. The following is an outline of the multidimensional aesthetic role of elegance in some current computer-based architectural practice where elegance in process is mirrored in its material manifestation.

The term 'aesthetics' here is not used synonymously with 'philosophy of the arts', but rather has to do with the perception of qualities generating feeling and emotion. Its use is as applicable to the natural world as it is to the artificial – a usage somewhat closer to its original coinage by Alexander

Ali Rahim and Hina Jamelle, Contemporary Architecture Practice, Reebok Flagship Store, Shanghai, China, 2005
An interior skin of vacuum-formed acrylic runs shoppers through a multipurpose satellite store.

Frank Gehry and Associates, Nationale-Nederlanden Building, Prague, Czech Republic, 1992–6
Gehry's dancing building at the River Vitava amid Old World wallflowers.

Baumgarten in his 1750 work *Aesthetica*, in which the aesthetic was understood as a form of confused, low-level perception. Elegance, like other aesthetic properties, has corresponding emotional fields that we can vaguely call pleasure (sometimes simply 'the agreeable' or delightful), noting how pleasures may vary in quantity and quality with any number of differences among its objects. But elegance also has a propensity towards elation and a lifting of the spirits towards a mood of civilised life. However temporary, the viewer may well be empowered by association with elegant art. With the emergence of elegance, it is as if digital technology has aided architects in rethinking utilitarian constraints peculiar to architecture as an art form, passing the inertia of theory, privileging aesthetics while displaying its process and having something to say in its material form about the role of aesthetics in architecture.

Lightness and fluidity might be two contingently related conditions of a certain species of elegance, one that has come to the fore by virtue of digital technology and so separates itself aesthetically from the elegance of other arts and architectures – Art Deco, too, having a claim to elegance on other grounds. This is lightness in the anti-gravitational sense, but it is related to the lightness that has darkness as its contrast, the medium of light being weightless or as close to weightlessness as it gets (it hardly needs reminding that digital technique is a matter of pressuring and so inflecting fields of light on computer monitors). Elegance is part of a

conceptual network that includes the likes of graceful, delicate, refined and balanced – what philosophers call aesthetic qualities, properties that are moving for the receptive subject. But it is iconic as well of an aesthetic Occam's razor, carrying with it nothing it does not need and so linking it to the myth of a minimalist architectural Modernism. Here, the idea of lightness (as in poker, 'The pot is light 50 dollars') designates a kind of lack or absence, drawing attention to what is not there as well as to the presence of something, and elegance, too, designates the extraneous missing. Elegance in this sense is neither gaudy nor ornate. As an aesthetic quality that presents itself in varying degrees of intensity and self-evidence, it emerges from the further aesthetic properties of lightness and fluidity.

Things in motion tend to appear lighter than things that are static, thus elegance is often associated with a kind of fluidity, smoothness of surface and style. In the case of architecture, the appearance of lightness contrasts sharply with its own inert condition, as if in denial of its own weight; the perception of lightness is the anti-gravitational illusion that architecture brings to its own reception. This line of thinking can gain support from the fact that prominent uses of software packages come to architecture from external sources, like CATIA from the motion-oriented industries, aerodynamics and automotive trades, and as another example, Maya, an animating software from the film industry.

Architecture, like still sculpture, can be elegant by its suggestion of fluidity and dynamism though it, too, is but a frozen moment and, by virtue of its elegance, appears to exhibit a kind of lightness. So, then, whatever else it is, elegance is a thin, bare-boned quality of refined organisation and efficiency and even in its complexity exhibits an appearance of lightness that is intensified by its suggestion of forms on the move.

But first a confession, what you might say is the elephant-in-the-room about elegance: it smacks of well-to-do-ness. 'Elegance' is not the first term we would use when thinking: blue collar. It is the tuxedoed Fred Astaire slipping frictionless across a posh and polished, luxurious nightclub floor – not Groucho Marx hunching around. It is Fred gesturing, in song and dance, but not Fred in comedic display stumbling through his own words, intimidated by the fabulous Ginger Rogers of his rarified screen partnership. Frank Gehry's elegant Nationale-Nederlanden Building (1992–6) at the Jiraskuv Bridge in Prague on the esplanade of the River Vitava is famously called the Ginger and Fred building. Critics have called it 'Gehry's Dancing Building' and praise the 'lightness and charm' in 'Gehry's elegant memorial'. Windows facing the river have been seen as 'bouncing and jumping'. Because of this class-oriented aspect of elegance, it was easy for Groucho and his brothers to deride the elegance foreign to most of their movie-going audience who had never spent a night at the opera.

In various versions of Cole Porter's *Did You Evah?*, part of the refrain goes: 'What a swell party, a swell party/A swelligant, elegant party this is!' On the *Red, Hot and Blue* CD, singing with Deborah Harrie, Iggy Pop sings, 'I hear they dismantled Big Bear/It wasn't elegant enough'. And there is no question from the tone and words of Cole Porter that elegance is a term of snobbery in *Did You Evah?*, poking fun at high-society manners.

The historical story of elegance contains this edge, meaning once 'dainty, fastidious, foppish', from as far back as the 16th century. But then some think there is a kind of elitism in architecture generally, a point that is relevant to the aesthetics of the art. Alan Colquhoun notes more conservative architecture's links with money and taste. He says: 'With architecture we are so bound to the sources of finance and power, it is much more difficult for the architect than for other artists to operate within an apparently autonomous subculture or to retain independence from bourgeois taste that has been the ambition of art since the early nineteenth century.'[1] Colquhoun may be forcing the point about the uniqueness of architecture, but there is a certain truth in what he says regarding the arts generally.

Elegance, like traditional architecture, is a package deal of a certain social dimension: with the pleasant aesthetic attributes that make it what it is comes a sense of refinement or luxury. The term 'class' is often used to designate some elegant entity or action. Here, it is easy to think of Aristotle's account of tragedy, which hangs on the inclusion of 'superior' characters as opposed to the 'low' roles in comedy.

One point of this detour into the language of social class is to introduce the notion of taste, or rather of good taste, and its objectivity – a well-entrenched issue in the history of philosophical aesthetics. Taste was once a powerful concept in thinking about the arts. It was then, though perhaps not now, a metaphorical rendering of the taste for whatever comes into contact with the human palate. For philosophers like David Hume (1711–76) it was something like a mental faculty that was intended to account for artistic excellence, foremost but not exclusively, the beautiful. And here was the issue that worried philosophers like Hume and Immanuel Kant (1724–1804): Was good taste, and hence the beautiful and the ugly or deformed, universal? Was there always and everywhere agreement on what was beautiful or artistically better and what not?

We can paraphrase this issue within our own discussion of elegance since, as recognition of an aesthetic property, the issue overlaps in certain ways. Hume's own tendency to say that judgements of artistic excellence are uniform or universal was simply falsified by the facts of human taste, not all of which was 'good'. Hume, sensitive to differences of class in his political writings, tries to explain these anomalies in a variety of ways: physiologically, as when one might have jaundice, or more relevantly a certain lack of experience or acquaintance with the arts not all of which is accessible to everyone, even in his native Scotland. Making the distinction between 'sentiment and judgement', Hume cites several no-contest comparisons (Milton vs Ogilby) generating evidence for standards, developed in part through artistic experience and 'a due attention to the object', hence opening the door for criticism

Zaha Hadid Architects, Zollhoff 3 Media Park, Dusseldorf, Germany, acrylic on canvas, London, 1993
A good representative painting of Hadid's marvellously fluid architecture.

Zaha Hadid, BMW Motorcar Company, Leipzig, Germany, 2005
Hadid's building seems to incorporate highways of light.

that is not merely a matter of in-born connoisseurship, but sometimes a matter for argument and debate.

Kant, on the other hand, to maintain the view that beauty is universal, makes the case that the beautiful must be a formal component of the aesthetic object as well as a subjective factor on the part of its perceiver. He insists that what needs to be adopted subjectively is to see the object from a disinterested point of view. Beauty for Kant is 'free' rather than 'dependent' when it does not fall under another concept. This is primarily Kant's formula of seeing the object as 'purposiveness without purpose', as if it had no quotidian role, and it helped to generate the formalism of Roger Fry, Clive Bell and Clement Greenberg who devalued, even dismissed, the content of art as beside the point. Since architecture in Kant's view was essentially related to purpose, architecture could not rank among the highest of the arts. The relation here between how one might think about elegance may be clear, but as neo-Kantian formalism has happily gone the way of other out-of-date theories, the

role of elegance in architecture as a result of digitalisation will require a richer and stronger analysis.

Philosophers are rarely on solid ground in any attribution of properties to things – of what really belongs to the world and what only appears (to us) to do so. Part of the historical problem has been the belief in the epistemological inaccessibility of the thing-in-itself, the world, as it is independent of human perception. One would think that what John Locke (1632–1704) called primary qualities – the 'powers' in objects to produce ideas or sensations in us such as extension (being extended in space), impenetrability, solidity and the like – were less subjective than what he called secondary qualities (redness, sweetness and so on), nothing in objects themselves except these powers to produce ideas of them in us. While for Locke primary qualities resemble the ideas they cause, secondary qualities are merely represented by our ideas of them, our own sense data in that respect having no claims to an allegedly material world.

The creativity of philosophers is not to be underestimated and the issue has spawned large numbers of permutations and combinations of solutions and dissolutions. But the problems regarding a complex property like elegance require yet another set of approaches from Lockean simples. Thus the 'faculty' of taste has been enlisted to function analogously to eyes for the visual or ears for the audible, but perhaps a bit closer to sense of humour for the comic.

So, then, the idea of an aesthetic property or quality has added another wrinkle to the issue of what belongs to the world, the universe of art objects or to nature. Being graceful or delicate (aesthetic qualities) requires a different epistemological analysis from roundness or roughness (so-called descriptive qualities). Theories have multiplied as to how aesthetic predicates are grounded as a result of the less problematic descriptive ones.

The 20th-century philosopher Frank Sibley reintroduced this problem in his classic 1959 essay 'Aesthetic Concepts' in which he argues that no amount of agreement about a work's nonaesthetic properties will guarantee uniformity of opinion regarding recognition of its emergent aesthetic ones, and in doing so reintroduces the tricky notion of taste. If elegance is descriptive of some architecture, and if the elegant contains not simply properties discernible by sense but also social attributions such as having a rarified character or being refined, then how can elegance appropriately signify something about architecture?

The answer to this question has something to do with the concept of meaning – the role of the meaning of a work in generating aesthetic responses. As Arthur Danto points out in his *The Abuse of Beauty*, the historical change from emphasising taste to emphasising meaning can be found in the difference between Kant and GWF Hegel (1770–1831). 'What Kant lacks,' Danto says, 'is the concept of meaning. Hegel requires art to have content ... Nothing more sharply distinguishes the philosophy of art in Kant and Hegel than the fact that taste is a central concept for Kant whereas it is discussed only to be dismissed by Hegel.'[2] Following Hegel, Danto distinguishes between instances of beauty where 'the meaning of the work is internally related to its aesthetic qualities'[3] and those where the aesthetic qualities of a work are only external, but not embodied as meaning. Early on, Modern architecture engaged meaning as an expression of social values in part as antidotal to 'modern life'. Simplicity of building became the manifesto for a reaction against too much and too many – a new complexity and eclecticism in the urban capitals of Europe – and in its minimalism advocated order in habit and habitation. The stripping of ornament and no-nonsense functionalism intending affordable dwelling for the working classes came to mean, perhaps ironically, corporate prestige in the second half of the 20th century. However, the exploration and impression of sensual response was not a strong point of architectural Modernism.

What we need to ask is whether the option of elegance, supervenient here upon the further qualities of lightness and fluidity generated in part by digitally employed techniques, belongs internally to what each work means. If not, although immediately recognised, elegance may lapse into a merely pleasing formalism. This is another way of asking whether elegance, and hence its conditions of lightness and fluidity embodied in work, are part of the thought the work expresses – in short, whether an elegant work is about elegance. Danto has often expressed the view that it is the 'aboutness' of a work and hence the requirement of interpretation that separates artworks from 'mere' real objects, even if they are perceptually indiscernible or nearly so.[4]

Thinking about the meaning embodied in an elegant work calls for a variety of debatable interpretations. The cover of the Rizzoli publication *Zaha Hadid: The Complete Work* is a dazzling display of a fictional compilation of Hadid's work that seems to be streaming rapidly in different directions. What we don't see is the base or grounding of these images. Much of Hadid's work, like her BMW Motorcar Company, is essentially about lightness and motion and the obvious elegance of her architecture manifests the very properties created in the digital processes intimately connected to their creation.

Another example is the interior of a flagship Reebok store in Shanghai's Xintiandi district by Ali Rahim and Hina Jamelle of Contemporary Architecture Practice. The Reebok brand strategy is 'Wear the Vector: Outperform', already underlining a product about direction, force and motion. And, as Rahim puts it, 'the store's users would literally inhabit a vector'. He goes on to say: 'The aim was to inflect the lower-intensity pressures, or arrangement of merchandise, with the higher-intensity pressures corresponding to the movement of people and goods. In other words, the interior would be activated by a flow from the exterior.'[5] Shopping, itself an exercise of taste, is nothing if not movement and selection, comparative consumption for the removal of merchandise soon to be replaced and redisplayed. (The etymological roots of 'elegance' tie it to the Latin *elegantem*, to choose or select.) Lightness in the Reebok store is also a result of the digitally processed selection of materials and structure that makes possible the flow of customer traffic.[6] The BMW and Reebok projects, like Rem Koolhaas' Prada Store in New York City, may be seen as part of a shift to brand sponsorship, where a not inexpensive product consumption is linked to manufactured 'good taste' in life as well as art.

Meaning in the arts is always 'meaning under an interpretation', and an interpretation is in part a theory of what the work is about. With the exception of residences tucked away on exclusive compounds, we have in architecture an artform often materially present to an involuntary public. Rather than embodying function or structure, this new elegance embodies, among other things, the elegance of its process. One way the mediation of digitalisation has contributed to the elegance of architecture is by making the fluidity of light part of the process of doing architecture and then inescapably part of the meaning of the work. It involves working on particle light fields that can be stretched seamlessly for continuity and flow or pressured to form shapes and openings that can make the direction of traffic, vehicular or pedestrian, an integral part of its formation.

In many cases an artwork is about how it came about. Jackson Pollock's paintings, for example, are about process as much as anything else.

The new elegance is a product of the lightness and fluidity intimate to its digital process and common to both the process and consequentially the formed building. The working of certain computer software has something to do with lightness and fluidity. Understanding each aspect of architecture, the digital process and the built product, is to understand an intimate connection between the two. Any explanation of a materially embodied elegance without including the elegance at work in its process would be seriously incomplete. The architecture can be understood as a trace of its process. This new elegance is aesthetically distinct from previous architectures and the degrees of separation between architectural styles can be linked to digital processing, which is as much a part of its meaning as its embedding qualities of lightness and fluidity.

Other architects, too, have been concerned with process in recent years, but in different ways. Peter Eisenman, for example, includes process in a series of textual strategies intended to suspend the privilege given to one of a pair of binary oppositions by traditional architecture. Additionally, his utilisation of trace, grafting and folding, and the injection of accident into his work makes process manifest even if not self-evident. However, let the results fall where they may, Eisenman is less concerned (or not at all) with aesthetic outcome than he is with a dislocation of a purported architectural essence. Here we have a dual aspect of reception theory, the immediacy of an aesthetic response and an interpreted meaning,

Take the case of Gehry's Guggenheim Museum in Bilbao, Spain, which is a juxtaposition of fluid fragments: the jumping, folding, bending, curving symphony of forms, the polished titanium mirrors changing with the reflected light of day and night, bring to the viewer a kind of celebration. It is as if a permanent metallic public fiesta has been parlayed into a precise ballet. Gehry thinks of it as billowing sails – a kind of movement at sea.

Gehry's museum, like the work of Hadid and Contemporary Architecture Practice, is elegant and anything but snobbery. It can be understood, I think, as a celebration of the arts, an embodiment of the spirit or mind of art in our time — a return to an architecture of what Nietzsche might have called being gay or joyful (as in his *The Gay Science*). The museum in Bilbao seems to embody traces of the digitalised screens that aided Gehry's initial sketches in bringing forth this civic focus on, and attitude towards, the arts.

Frank Gehry and Associates, Guggenheim Museum, Bilbao, Spain, 1997
Coloured by the light of day and night, Gehry's flowing titanium facade streams around a grand exterior stairway.

Aerospace technologies in the service of Gehry's 'maritime' sculptural wonder.

Each of the projects discussed here houses expensive items that carry the themes of elegance mentioned earlier. Furthermore, they join, perhaps reflect, a culture with shorter spans of attention, demands for swift responses in work and play and fleeting imagery, in practising the rituals of taste in its daily movements. The presence of elegance helps to deconstruct architecture's traditional essence of solidity, strength and weight, and with the shedding of the appearance of architecture's gravity comes a move towards a popular notion of elegance.

If the above works are exemplars of digital techniques that have come to occupy an architecture, then it should be clear that elegance is not the result of taste alone – as even the aesthetic properties possessed by a work are determined under an interpretation. Taste becomes a partner of meaning in the experience of elegance. Elegance becomes a supervening, rather complex and compound aesthetic property, subjectively dependent upon the further aesthetic properties lightness and fluidity, which may further be supervening upon other determinations emerging uniquely through digital techniques and architectural selection.[7] ⚙

Notes
1. Alan Colquhoun, 'Postmodernism and Structuralism: A Retrospective Glance', *Assemblage*, No. 5, February 1988, pp 7–8.
2. Arthur Danto, *The Abuse of Beauty: Aesthetics and the Concept of Art*, Open Court (Chicago, IL), 2003, p 67.
3. Ibid, p 97.
4. Arthur Danto, *The Transfiguration of the Commonplace: A Philosophy of Art*, Harvard University Press (Cambridge, MA, and London), 1981.
5. Ali Rahim, *Catalytic Formations: Architecture and Digital Design*, Routledge (London), 2005 p 52.
6. Rahim describes the material as follows: 'The store is composed of a prefabricated semi-monocoque aluminum shell hung from the structure of an existing building. The interior skin of the store is made of clear vacuum-formed acrylic.' Ibid, p 53.
7. Thanks to Jeff Kipnis for a fine conversation about an earlier draft of this paper.

Material Elegance

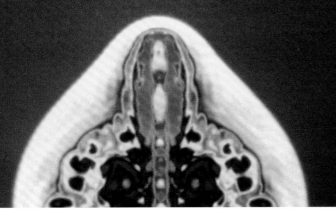

In the everyday, elegance is a wholly subjective attribute. Whether we deem someone to be 'elegant' is entirely dependent on our own personal perception of their outward appearance. Here, **Manuel DeLanda** provides for architecture an objective interpretation of the elegant or smart solution in which 'there is a measurable economy of means to achieve a certain outcome'. Through a brief historical survey, he traces an empirical tradition of material elegance.

There are many meanings of the word 'elegant', some more subjective some more objective. Elegance may be said to be in the eye of the beholder, or to be defined by the customs and habits of a cultural tradition, and thus to have very little to do with objectivity. On the other hand, we may use the word to refer to objective processes, whether natural or human, in which there is a measurable economy of means to achieve a certain outcome.

It is in this latter sense that we may speak of 'material elegance'. But even if we accept that there is a certain objective sense in which the production of an outcome, or the achievement of a goal, can be said to be elegant if it makes the most economic use of resources, if it produces the most with the least, there are still many ways to approach the question. Subjectivity and tradition can still impinge on the

choice of approach, restricting or enlarging the space of possible ways to think about the question.

A brief historical survey of material elegance in Western science reveals how this space of possible approaches has been progressively enlarged from its relatively narrow beginnings in the 17th century to the present day.

Our survey starts in 1662, when Pierre de Fermat first postulated that light propagates between two points so as to minimise travel time. Other 'least principles' were added to Fermat's in the centuries that followed (least action, least effort, least resistance, least potential energy), all of which expressed an elegant use of means to generate form. Some of the discoverers of least principles were so impressed by the elegance nature seemed to display in producing its effects that they believed they had found a proof of the existence of God: if

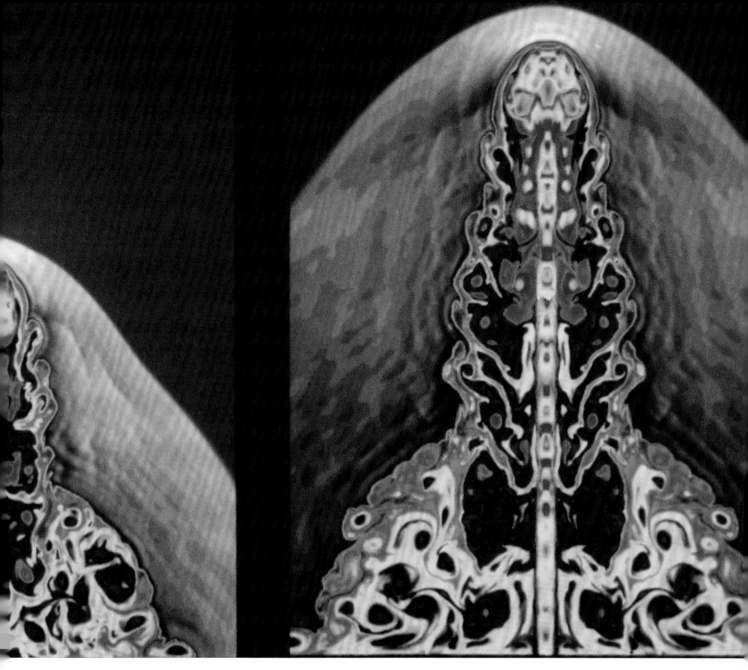

Computer model of turbulence in a supersonic jet, displaying the elegant patterns of vortices within vortices for three different intensities of the driving parameter.

the supreme being possessed a supreme rationality, rationality being the ability to match means to ends, then he surely would have elegantly economised on the means he used to achieve his ends. In this view every natural process that produces a material form would be an optimization process, and the resulting perfect forms would be a natural reflection of the perfection of their creator. An argument like this was used, for example, by Pierre Louis Moreau de Maupertuis, who discovered the least action principle around 1744.

If these theological speculations were all that least principles had to offer, they would have died together with God in the 19th century. But they did not for two reasons. The first is that although not every form-producing process is an optimisation process, there are indeed objective processes governed by the tendency to minimise or maximise a certain

physical quantity. In other words, while optimisation is only subjectively (or traditionally) universal, it is fully objective in some areas of reality. The second reason is that, in addition to theological speculation, some of the people involved in the discovery of least principles produced something more enduring: a mathematical procedure to deal with minima and maxima, that is, with singularities. Leonhard Euler's 18th-century creation of this 'software', today referred to as 'the calculus of variations', was indeed an achievement with long-lasting consequences.

Fermat's basic insight may be summarised as follows: if we knew the start and end points of a given light ray, and if we could form the set of all possible paths, straight ones, wavy ones, crooked ones, that joined these two points, the path actually realised in nature would be the one taking the least

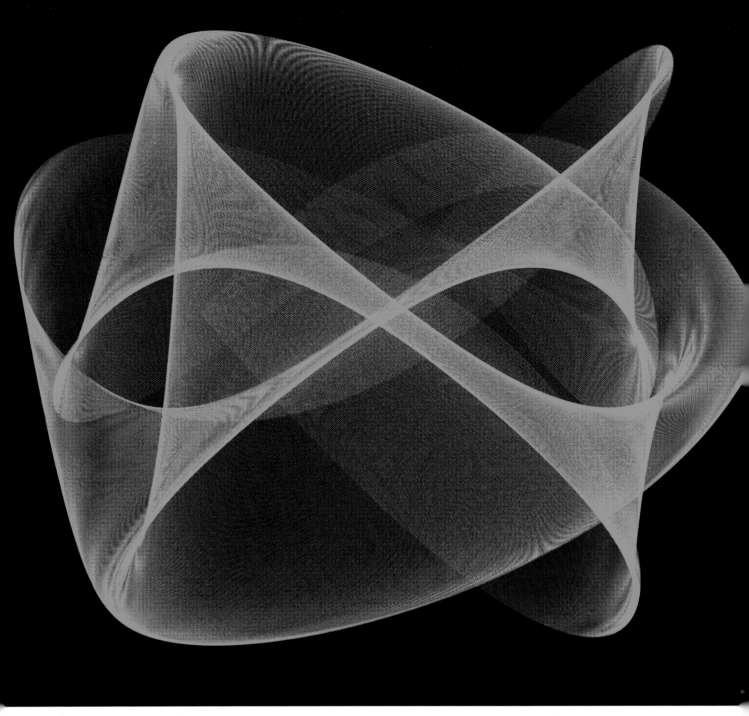

Mathematical model based on a sine wave.

amount of time. But if this was to become a general method, it was necessary to find a way to specify the set of possible paths so that it contained all possibilities. This could be achieved by 'parametrising' the paths; that is, by generating the paths through the variation of a single parameter. The problem is that there are many physical problems in which the possibilities cannot be parametrised by a discrete set of variables.

Euler's calculus of variations solved this problem, at least for the case of mathematical models that use differential equations. But, more importantly, it also influenced several generations of physicists, including such luminaries as Lagrange and Hamilton, who began to use variational ideas in novel ways. By the mid-19th century Hamilton had shown that

all classical processes, whether optical, gravitational or mechanical, could be modelled using a single least principle: the tendency of material processes to minimise the difference between kinetic and potential energy. In terms of economy of means, this unification of all classical physics under a single principle was indeed a highly elegant solution.

Let's pause for a moment to consider the significance of this achievement. The sense of elegance in a Hamiltonian equation derives from its simplicity. But simplicity has at least two meanings. The first is related to the famous principle known as Occam's razor, which recommends shaving off all unnecessary embellishments in a theory or model, getting rid of all redundancies, so as to be able to see more clearly its basic analytic structure. It recommends, in short, an economy of means in the achievement of conceptual goals. In this sense simplicity is indeed related to material elegance. However, there is another sense of the word in which 'simplicity' means nothing more than 'familiarity': one uses certain equations not because they are the simplest means to build a model that captures reality, but because they have become routine and are therefore the simplest ones to use. This routinisation is precisely what entrenched the idea that all processes are optimisation processes, and what transformed the concept into a secular myth. The same overgeneralisation made a myth of its subjective counterpart, the concept of an 'optimizing rationality'.

From the point of view of material elegance, the main damage caused was the entrenchment of the assumption that all complexity is inelegant – that it is mere complicatedness, the kind of complexity that can be eliminated through a proper use of Occam's razor. Yet there are forms of irreducible complexity that display an elegance of their own, but which have been historically marginalised (until the second half of the 20th century) because of their unfamiliarity.

Thus, the achievements of variational thought cannot be properly evaluated in terms of simplicity alone. Rather, it is the very concept of a space of possibilities (such as the set of all possible light rays joining start and end points) that matters. Or better yet, the structure of such a space, a structure given in terms of singularities. A possibility space structured by a single optimum (for example, a minimum of potential energy) would indeed indicate that a simple process of optimisation is behind the genesis of a given form, and the elegance of that form will be related to the existence of that unique singularity. But possibility spaces, we now know, come in all kinds of flavours, the ones possessing a single optimum being only a particular case. This discovery came about thanks to the work of other mathematicians, starting with Henri Poincare at the end of the 19th century, who brought topological resources to bear on the study of possibility spaces, revealing an unsuspected and highly elegant complexity.

Like Euler, Poincare was interested in studying the behaviour of differential equations or, more exactly, of the solutions to those equations. But unlike Euler, Poincare did not confine his studies to equations in which the possibility space (the space of all solutions) was structured by a single optimum. Using topological manifolds to model the space of solutions (a space known as 'phase space') he was able to discover a richer repertoire of singularities. The kind of point singularities with which variational thinkers were familiar came now in different forms, depending on the behaviour of solutions nearby and, more importantly, they came in bunches, giving rise to possibility spaces with multiple optima.

Poincare also discovered that zero-dimensional singularities (points) were only part of the repertoire. One-dimensional singularities, lines bent so as to form a closed loop, were another possibility. If point-singularities

represented a steady state for a physical process, these loops (called 'limit cycles' or 'periodic attractors') captured the behaviour of rhythmic processes – processes that sequence through a series of states over and over again. That the possibility space for a process had the capacity to spontaneously generate rhythmic behaviour by simply attracting the process to a cyclic singularity was clearly a sign of economy of means. Suddenly, all kinds of periodic behaviour, from the convection cells formed by winds or lava flows to the metabolic cycles of simple organisms, became explainable by a single topological feature of an abstract possibility space.

The material elegance with which cyclic singularities endow physical and biological processes is best exhibited when considering not single oscillating entities, but large numbers of them. Periodic behaviour may be divided into two classes depending on whether the source of the rhythm is endogenous or exogenous. The ebb and flow of the tide is a good example of the latter, the moon's gravitational pull being the exogenous cause, while processes driven by a periodic attractor exemplify the former: they have their own internal source of energy and are capable of maintaining a stable rhythm even in the presence of small shocks and noise. These are referred to as 'self-sustained oscillators', and their most important property is their ability to spontaneously synchronise with each other by a mutual adjustment of their internally generated rhythms. An example of mutual adjustment is the spectacular displays of thousands of fireflies emitting light simultaneously, as observed along the tidal rivers of Malaysia or Thailand. But the neurons in our brains may also become spontaneously synchronised, as may the photons in a laser beam. Given the complexity inherent in getting thousands, if not millions, of entities to beat at the same rhythm, the economy of means through which this is achieved in all kinds of inorganic and organic processes is surely an expression of material elegance.

Besides periodic attractors, Poincare glimpsed the existence of a stranger kind, a type of singularity that may be pictured as the result of repeatedly folding and stretching a simple loop. To perform these transformations one has to leave the two-dimensional phase space in which cyclic singularities live, much as one has to use the extra space offered by three dimensions in order to twist a long piece of paper into a Möbius strip. The result of folding and stretching the loop, however, does not ever reach three dimensions, but stays at an intermediate, or fractal, dimension between two and three.

Fractals, in Poincare's time, were literally considered mathematical monsters, anomalous curves and surfaces that had the status of mere curiosities, like the exhibits at a freak show. So Poincare's brief look at these complex singularities horrified him. Even in our own time, their complexity and internal divergence have led people to give them the wrong name: chaos. A quick look at a chaotic or fractal attractor, such as the Lorenz attractor or the Rössler attractor, however, suggests an intriguing elegance behind these singularities, something far removed from the randomness that the word 'chaos' suggests. But looks are deceiving and, at any rate, the definition of material elegance in terms of economy of means has nothing to do with visual appearance. Thus, to understand why these strange singularities are important it is necessary to focus on their topological role of structuring a space of possibilities.

Phase spaces can come in any number of dimensions, one for every 'degree of freedom' of the physical process being modelled. This expression refers to the number of relevant ways a process is free to change, or to the number of changing properties that define its states. The more dimensions a phase space has, the more 'room' there is in it; that is, the larger the number of possible states for the process in question. Singularities of any kind are able to generate spontaneous order in an economic way simply by reducing the number of possibilities or, more exactly, by giving to these possibilities different probabilities of being realised. In a phase space with no attractors, every possible state is equally likely to be realised, so the trajectory that represents series of states for the process being modelled will aimlessly wander throughout phase space. The process that such a phase space models, in turn, will exhibit no spontaneous emergence of order, being a truly random process. But if an attractor is present, the state it represents will have a much higher probability of being realised, the trajectory will cease to wander around and will be typically attracted to the singularity, a fact that will be manifested in reality as the emergence of orderly form. (Attractors are, in fact, fully deterministic, but when there are many of them, which attractor is realised becomes a probabilistic question).

This is the real, topological source of elegance in material processes. Thus, despite the fact that a chaotic attractor is internally divergent, which means that it is able to defy prediction by being ultrasensitive to minor changes in initial conditions, it may still generate order if it is 'small' relative to the size of phase space. A chaotic attractor with dimensions between two and three, for example, inhabiting a hundred-dimensional phase space, would still reduce enormously the available possibilities, and the process being modelled will look anything but random. Rather, it would be a manifestation of a highly elegant solution to the problem of generating quasi-periodic oscillations that can adapt to different circumstances. Such oscillations, some researchers have found, may characterise the human heart, which if forced to oscillate too regularly can become brittle and fail.

In addition to its dimensions, the phase space of a given process is characterised by a number of control parameters. A given process may, for example, have temperature as one of its degrees of freedom. But the process may take place in an environment which also has a given temperature. This external temperature is incorporated into a model as a control parameter. Control parameters can serve to connect several phase spaces together. Imagine a phase space divided into four or five point attractors, and a control parameter that switches the system from one attractor to another when it changes. That is, the system will be in a different steady state for different values of the parameter.

Now, imagine a separate phase space inhabited by a single periodic attractor, but which is connected to the control parameter of the first. As the second system cycles through its own states, it changes the values of the first system's parameter with the consequence that the system cycles through its point attractors over and over again. This set of two coupled phase spaces could model a simple organism that cycles through a series of states (waking, feeling hungry, eating, feeling satiated, sleeping) every day. These coupled systems, called hierarchical systems, can be made as complex as one wishes, with many state spaces coupled either serially or in parallel, and undergoing complex transformations called bifurcations at each level. A bifurcation is an event that occurs when a control parameter reaches a critical point and one distribution of singularities mutates into distribution. The relatively large combinatorial space that this opens up is a rich source of complexity in such models, a complexity that preserves the material elegance of the system.

Thus we have come a long way since the simple minima and maxima of the calculus of variations. But this does not mean that the simple possibility spaces first explored by Euler are obsolete. Many real life form-generating processes do happen to have a possibility space structured by a simple singularity, such as a minimum of energy. The form-generating processes behind soap bubbles (which minimise surface tension) or crystals (which minimise bonding energy) are good illustrations. The processes that generate these geometrical forms may be viewed as searching a possibility space until they reach the singularity. Hence, they can be used by artists as form-finding procedures. The most famous example of this in architecture is the work performed since the 1950s at the Institute for Lightweight Structures in Stuttgart, under the inspiration and guidance of Frei Otto. Otto is best known for his use of soap film as a means to find minimal forms. Unconstrained, soap film will always find a sphere, but constrained (and the designer's role here is to define the proper constraints) it can find a variety of minimal surfaces such as the hyperbolic paraboloids that Otto used for his tent-like roof designs.

On the other hand, to concentrate on possibility spaces with a single point attractor clearly disregards all the inherent complexity that, as topologists have found, characterises phase spaces, not to mention the combinatorial complexity of hierarchical systems. Biology, particularly the biology of multicellular organisms, is one field in which many possibility spaces characterise separate but coupled levels of scale. The dynamics of interacting cells have one possibility space, the interactions between organs have another, and the entire organism has yet another. These three levels are clearly coupled, with the singularities governing the dynamics of organs linked to the control parameters of cells, and with the organs' own control parameters coupled to the singularities of

The Lorenz attractor. This was the first chaotic attractor to be systematically studied. Its elegant symmetry shows how misleading the term 'chaos' can be, focusing on the unpredictability of the trajectories in the attractor instead of on its complex and beautiful internal structure.

the entire organism. In addition to this complexity is the fact that, thanks to the existence of genetic information, the entire ensemble of possibility spaces can evolve.

Evolution itself is a search process in the possibility space of an entire reproductive community of organisms. The genetic algorithm, a virtual-reality version of biological evolution, is indeed classified as a search algorithm. Compared to the relatively simple random walks that the molecules in soap film use to find the singularity representing a minimum of surface tension, evolutionary walks are much more effective since they occur in parallel (the entire reproductive community searches the space simultaneously), though they are much slower as each step of the walk takes an entire generation (thus, the search is not performed by a single reproductive community, but by many

generations of such communities). Nevertheless, when implemented in computers, evolutionary searches can be quite efficient and may be capable of finding forms in several coupled state spaces at once; that is, new cell types, new organs and new organisms.

This should not make us lose our appreciation for the simple possibility spaces that Euler first explored, nor for those architects like Frei Otto who have implemented form-finding procedures in those spaces. But it should fill us with wonder at what other elegant form-finding processes may be waiting to be discovered. ⅅ

Frozen Void

The Elegant Affect of the Evolved Object

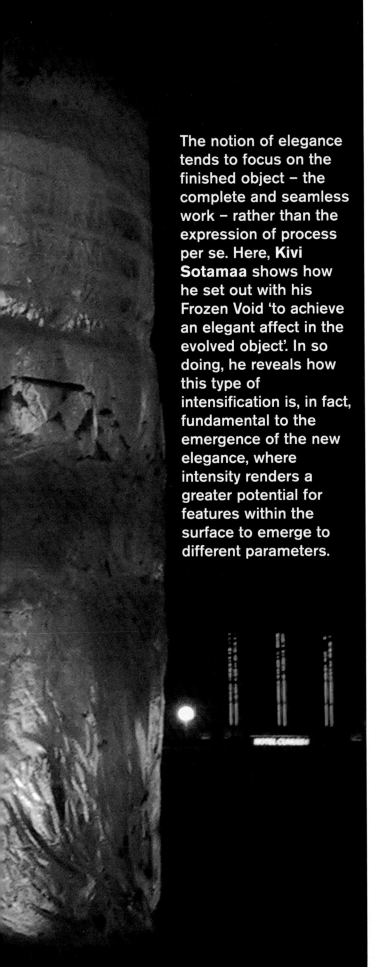

The notion of elegance tends to focus on the finished object – the complete and seamless work – rather than the expression of process per se. Here, **Kivi Sotamaa** shows how he set out with his Frozen Void 'to achieve an elegant affect in the evolved object'. In so doing, he reveals how this type of intensification is, in fact, fundamental to the emergence of the new elegance, where intensity renders a greater potential for features within the surface to emerge to different parameters.

Elegant projects do not reveal the process of their formation. The complexity and depth of their formal and material articulation is such that they cannot be 'read'. They produce new rhythms and sensations of emergent formations – think of staring at a cloud. The Frozen Void was an attempt to reoriginate[1] such an experience into architecture, or sculpture, to achieve an elegant affect[2] in the evolved object.

A cylindrical object of ice approximately 4 metres (13 feet) in height and diameter, the Frozen Void ice building contained a naturally evolved void that could be entered by people. It was designed using a natural form-finding process – freezing water. Project collaborator Ernesto Neto believed the process of freezing water in a mould to be like baking a sculpture; that is, just pouring the water in a 'negative oven' and waiting for the void to emerge. However, I saw the process as a computer algorithm, which is essentially a recipe, a finite set of well-defined instructions for accomplishing a task, such as developing a form. Either way, the ice building was entirely generated by the mould and the automated form-finding process.

Neto and myself both deploy algorithmic physical and computational processes in our work, but neither wishes those processes to be 'read' in the end result. Neto builds his sculptures out of spandex fabric that naturally finds mathematical minimal surface geometries akin to the structures of Frei Otto. However, unlike Otto he avoids calling attention to the forces that govern them, and uses translucency, colour and representation – loose affiliations to bodily forms – to distract attention from the construction logic. I explore algorithmic processes because of their power to produce continuous variation of topological forms. Such forms can be very precise in terms of their affect, and simultaneously suggestive, open to interpretation. They do not produce differences in kind – typological differences[3] – but generate differences in intensities that operate more like human emotions. They create moods and atmospheres[4] that appeal to our feelings as opposed to our intellect.

Process-based architectural works often include an identifiable geometrical primitive that has travelled through space, leaving a trace. A canonic example is Peter Eisenman's Aronoff Center in Cincinnati. And contemporary examples are the many digitally generated designs that deploy mutating iterations of a form. In most cases, the traces call viewers' attention to the process. However, some more recent work has reached a level of complexity that escapes 'reading'. For example, Hernan Diaz Alonso's iterative forms create the sensation of a rhythm, and Ali Rahim and Hina Jamelle's

---

SOTAMAA architecture & design, Frozen Void, Kemi, Finland, 2004
Exterior view. Frozen Void was an ice building realised in collaboration with Brazilian sculptor Ernesto Neto. A cylindrical steel-reinforced plywood mould was sealed with a plastic tarmac and filled with 50 cubic metres (1,766 cubic feet) of water from the Bay of Finland. The water was left to freeze for two weeks before the mould was opened. A solid monolith of ice was revealed. On its outside surface were traces of the folds and ripples of the plastic tarmac, and the inside was filled with unfrozen water.

inside, the massive solidity of the exterior was gone. The space was dreamlike, immaterial and weightless. It resulted simply from the interplay of the natural forces with the water contained by the walls of the mould.

The temperatures of the different days were registered as ledges on the wall. The colour of the surface changed as the colour of the water pumped from the sea had varied. The thickness alternated according to the outside temperature and directions of the wind on the site. Some ice was white, almost like snow, and some was so clear that one could see outside.

patterns produce figurative formations. Both affects have the power to turn the viewer's attention away from the formative process towards new emergent phenomena.

The challenge in the design of the Frozen Void was to hide the process because, whether computer algorithm or freezing water, it inevitably encourages observers to focus on the traces, to 'read' them, instead of experiencing the architecture emotionally. Formally driven, process-based design often seems 'difficult'[5] because it stages an analytical, cold and distanced experience as opposed to the 'easy',[6] immediate and emotional. In order to foreground the affective powers of our ice building, the process needed to be in the background.

Frozen Void was a success in that, though viewers could sense the mathematics behind its formations, they could not decipher them. There was no geometrical primitive, no construction details, seams, joints, trusses or surfaces to make the structure legible, just a continuously differentiated skin of ice that refracted and reflected light. In the void, one quickly became distracted, engulfed in the pure atmosphere of the space. And it was in this state of distracted attention,[7] staring at the ice, that form and pattern emerged out of the chaos, and the architecture lost all of its traces of process to become entirely about new affects. It contained no history, no messages, no meaning, but when experienced by the viewer produced new meaning, messages and feelings.

The sensation produced was akin to that of the sublime – the experience of nothingness in the face of the force and complexity of a natural formation.[8] Many naturally evolved environments and objects are a result of such a complex set of forces, where one can only sense the presence of logic and not fully comprehend, or 'read', it. Imagine staring at a waterfall, a fire, a slot canyon or the snakeskin surface of the ocean at sunset. Today's digital, algorithmic design processes enable designs whose sensations rival those of evolved objects and environments. Thus elegance is achieved when a complex architectural object foregrounds its affective powers and delivers its affects effortlessly. The elegant architectural object embodies process, without calling attention to it. ◾

Notes

1. Jeffrey Kipnis has introduced the term 'reorigination' to architectural discourse as an alternative to 'representation'. See Jeffrey Kipnis, Re-originating Diagrams', in Peter Eisenman, *Feints*, Skira (Milan), 2006, pp 193–203.
2. The term 'elegant affect' has been used intentionally here. Though this may seem grammatically incorrect, it points to the experience the architecture produces in the beholder, rather than the 'effect'.
3. Jesse Reiser and Nanako Umemoto have said that they explore differences in intensity as opposed to differences in kind in order to foreground the affective powers of their work. See Jesse Reiser, *Atlas of Novel Tectonics*, Princeton Architectural Press (Princeton, NJ), 2006.
4. Jefrrey Kipnis has theorised the importance of mood and atmosphere in architecture. See Jeffrey Kipnis, op cit.
5. Robert Somol introduced the concepts of 'difficult' and 'easy' in his discussion of architecture of 'form' versus architecture of 'shape'. The use of these terms in this essay deviates from Somol's, in proposing that there are both 'difficult' and 'easy' forms in terms of people's experiences. See Robert Somol, '12 Reasons to get back into shape', in Rem Koolhaas, *Content*, Taschen (Cologne), 2003.
6. Ibid.
7. 'Distracted attention' was first discussed by Walter Benjamin in 'The work of art in the age of the mechanical reproduction', in Walter Benjamin and Harry Zohn, *Illuminations*, Schocken (New York), 1968, pp 217–52.
8. Immanuel Kant identified two types of sublime: the 'mathematical sublime' and the 'dynamical sublime'. The latter is found in nature – the experience of nothingness in the face of the force and complexity of a waterfall. According to Kant, the 'mathematical sublime' emerges over the dynamical sublime as something superior to nature. Gilles Deleuze proposes another role of the 'mathematical sublime'. He says that ideas are not superior or transcendental to nature, but immanent to experience itself, 'suprasensible': 'Ideas reveal the forces or intensities that lie behind sensations.' For Deleuze, the 'mathematical sublime' is something inherent in the human experience of the sublime in nature. See Gilles Deleuze, *Francis Bacon: The Logic of Sensation*, Continuum International Publishing Group-Mansell, 2004.

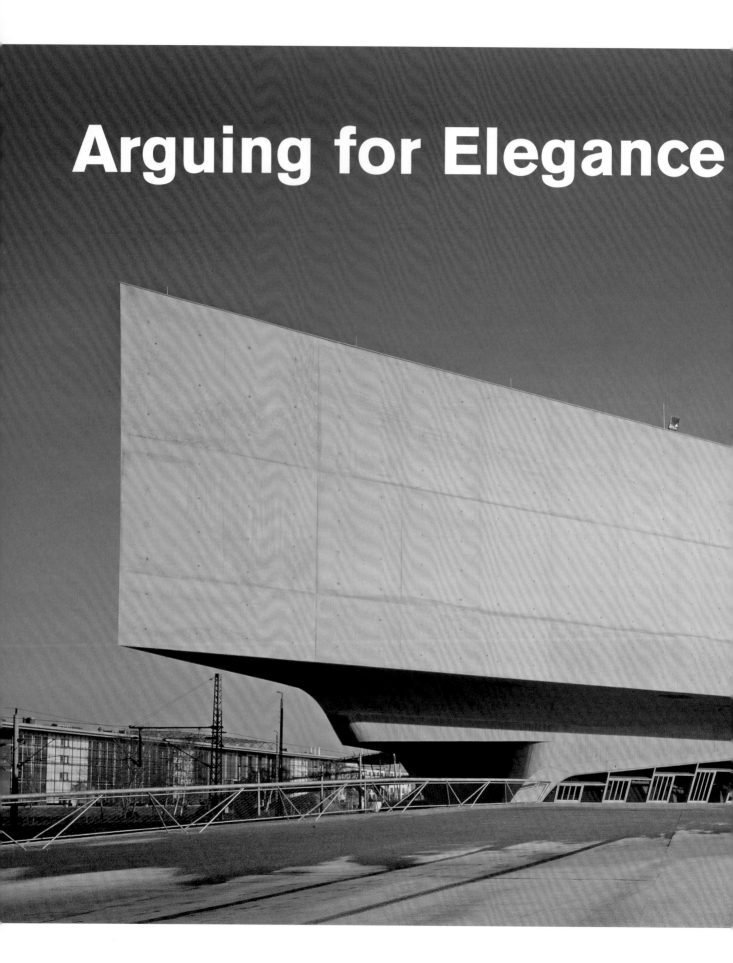

Arguing for Elegance

Patrik Schumacher of Zaha Hadid Architects describes how elegance in architecture thrives on and articulates complexity. For elegance to be fully expressed in any work, it must be mastered and refined throughout the building and construction process. This entails the refinement of spatial and structural organisation and the integration of all building systems that are systemic, inflecting and adapt to each other, providing an overall intelligence of assembly.

Zaha Hadid Architects, Phaeno Science Centre, Wolfsburg, Germany, 2005
The recently completed science museum in Wolfsburg is the virtuoso masterpiece in the articulation of complex continuities that can be followed all the way through the building. The whole building is inscribed within a rigid trapezoid, its angles adapted to the site conditions.
Lead designer: Christos Passos
Design team: Sara Klomps, Gernot Finselbach, Helmut Kinzler

Elegance speaks for itself. In everyday life it suggests sophistication, taste and refinement. It is an unquestioned value of immediate appeal and in no need for argument.

However, as a new explicit watchword claiming to guide the next stage of avant-garde architecture, it constitutes a provocation. And it is precisely this mainstream appeal of elegance that runs counter to the very self-conception of any avant-gardism. In fact, the pursuit of elegance is most probably incompatible with radical newness. On the count of radicalism the pursuit of strangeness and the construction of 'abstract machines'[1] is more productive than anything one might expect from the pursuit of elegance. However, innovation involves more than radical newness. Mutation is to be followed by selection, recombination and refinement before the avant-garde can release its results to mainstream reproduction.[2]

The time is ripe. We have reached the final stages of the current cycle of avant-gardist innovation: folds and blobs are heading mainstream. The escape from the rarefied realm of academia and art – the twin feeding grounds for potential innovations in architecture and design – should not be denigrated. What else should be the destiny and purpose of the avant-garde? Its function is to advance the development of the discipline. Avant-garde and mainstream are two complementing sides of a single evolution: architectural progress. Like any evolutionary process, this one has differentiated specific evolutionary mechanisms for mutation (avant-garde), selection (critics and early adopters) and reproduction (mainstream profession).

Ali Rahim and Hina Jamelle are rightly arguing that the scene is set for a phase of refinement rather than a phase of further radical newness. 'Elegance' is perhaps the most pertinent slogan for this phase. Other candidates and contenders might step forward, but there can be no doubt about the need for effective slogans to direct and cohere our creative energies into an effective collective effort.

The immediate appeal of elegance is certainly an asset in the push towards the mainstream. The current theoretical emptiness of elegance is also an asset rather than a liability. Elegance is certainly a much more clever choice than the traditional theoretical heavyweight 'beauty'. While beauty is so loaded and contested that it will stir up a burdensome deadload of theoreticians wasting our time with irrelevant quarrels about the essence of beauty, 'elegance' is lite, a theoretical virgin territory, giving plenty of space to manoeuvre, allowing us to elaborate all the specific semantic connections, connotations and nuanced demarcations we require to define this concept for our purposes and harness its positive energy to push the particular trajectory of avant-garde architecture at this current juncture. What follows is the attempt to help in the forging of such a particular notion of elegance.

Elegance is a mainstream value with widespread application in many arenas. There is nothing new or original about using this term in the architectural arena. What is original and provocative is the attempt to push it into the forefront of the current avant-garde architectural trend and to do this by giving it a well-defined thrust and theoretical underpinning.

Theory of Elegance

The elegance being referred to is not the elegance of minimalism. Minimalist elegance thrives on simplicity. The elegance being promoted here instead thrives on complexity, and achieves a visual reduction of an underlying complexity that is thereby sublated rather than eliminated. Elegance thus articulates complexity.

This new theory of elegance in contemporary architecture has two distinct components:

1 descriptive: the elaboration of a descriptive language that provides the resources to distinguish and characterise the style in question and the particular agenda of its refinement
2 argumentative: the stipulation of form–function relationships and the formulation of hypotheses about the social efficacy and pertinence of 'elegant architecture' in the context of contemporary societal challenges.[3]

Attributed to a person, elegance suggests the effortless display of sophistication. We also talk about an elegant solution to a complex problem. In fact only if the problem is complex and difficult does the solution deserve the attribute 'elegant'. While simplistic solutions are pseudo-solutions, the elegant solution is marked by an economy of means by which it conquers complexity and resolves (unnecessary) complications. It is this kind of connotation that we would like to harness. An elegant building or urban design should therefore be able to manage considerable complexity without descending into disorder.

We might adopt the language of system theory and speak of more or less complex systems. We might distinguish two types of items that might differentiate/compose a system: elements and subsystems (collections of related/connected elements). With respect to the measure of (ordered) complexity, we might distinguish several dimensions:

1 the number and diversity of distinguishable items within the complex
2 the density and diversity of relationships between distinguishable items
3 relations between ordered sets of elements (correlations)
4 relations between relations (systems of relations).

An elegant composition displays a high level of complexity in all dimensions, including the higher dimensions 3 and 4, which imply a move from complexity to ordered complexity. As ordered complexity, the elegant composition is highly differentiated, yet this differentiation is rule governed, based on a systematic set of lawful correlations that are defined between the differentiated elements and subsystems. Such correlations integrate and (re-)establish a visible coherence and unity across the differentiated system.[4]

Within the sharp-edged trapezoid, everything flows and melds without corners. The ground surface is moulded into an artificial topography that registers and receives the cones that carry the building.

Elegance and Organisation

Two parallel applications of the concept of complexity need to be distinguished in our domain of reference: the underlying complexity of the institutional arrangements and life-processes on the one hand needs to be distinguished from the complexity of the spatial arrangements and architectural forms that help to organise and articulate those life-processes on the other hand. The underlying social complexity has to be somehow translated into the spatial complexity of an architectural complex. The concept of organisation operates at a level of abstraction that encompasses both domains. It is possible to elaborate types, patterns, systems and dimensions of organisation that can guide both the analysis of the (complex) social processes as well as the synthesis of the appropriate (complex) spatial forms. Complex social organisation is to be registered, facilitated and expressed by elegant spatial formations.

The primary argument here is that, understood in this way elegance facilitates orientation within a spatial complex arrangement and thus ensures the legibility of a complex social formation. Again, elegance articulates complexity. And the articulation of complexity prevents perplexity.

Elegance as Second Nature

It is the sense of law-governed complexity that assimilates this work to the forms and spaces we perceive in organic as well as in inorganic natural systems, where all forms are the result of lawfully interacting forces. Just like natural systems, elegant compositions are so highly integrated that they cannot easily be decomposed into independent subsystems – a major point of difference in comparison with the modern design paradigm of clear separation of functional subsystems. In fact, the exploitation of natural forms such as landscape formations or organic morphologies as a source domain for analogical transference into architecture makes a constructive contribution to the development of this new paradigm and language of architecture.

Frei Otto went a step further and literally harnessed the lawfulness of physical systems as a form-finding procedure to generate his design-morphology. The results have been striking. Lars Spuybroek has described these processes as 'material computing'.[5] Such elegant compositions resist decomposition, just like their natural models.

A specific aspect of this overall lawful and integrated nature of elegance is the capacity of elegant compositions to adapt to complex urban contexts. Adaptive capacity or adaptation is another key ambition of the contemporary avant-garde trend that might suggest comparison with natural organic systems. An architectural system that has an enhanced capacity to adapt to its environment will result in an intricate artefact-context ensemble that has sublated initial contradictions into a new complex synthesis that further enhances the overall sense of sophisticated elegance.

Designing Elegance

This effect, which in nature emerges through self-organisation, has to be elaborately constructed in sustained design efforts, guided by appropriate recipes and principles.

Robert Venturi made an early contribution by formulating a compositional principle that is useful here. His notion of the 'difficult whole' is concerned with the compositional integration of diversity: 'It is the difficult unity through inclusion rather than the easy unity through exclusion.[6] One of the specific techniques Venturi has identified is the technique he terms 'inflection'. 'By inflecting towards something outside themselves, the parts contain their own linkage.'[7] He identified this technique and its integrative effect in Baroque architecture, in comparison with the more additive structure of Renaissance compositions where each subsystem rests complete within itself. In contrast, Baroque inflection achieves the integration of parts (subsystems) by means of imposing an overarching curvature that leaves the part asymmetrical/incomplete, requiring the other complementary parts to continue and complete the curvature.

The concept of inflection can be generalised so that elegance requires that the layers and subsystems of a complex composition are mutually inflected. Every new element or new layer that enters the complex will both inflect the overall composition and will in turn be inflected. Elegance can never result from a merely additive complication.[8]

Computing Elegance

Current digital modelling tools are able to facilitate integrative effects: lofting, spline networks, soft bodies, working with force fields and so on. Morphing – the ultimate effect of film animation technology – has been an often emulated paradigm for achieving the continuity of the differentiated.

There is an inevitable, powerful relationship between the new digital tools (such as animation software), compositional tropes and stylistic characteristics. Intensive coherence (Jeff Kipnis), pliancy, multiple affiliations and intricacy (Greg Lynn) are some of the concepts coined to describe the compositional ambitions that emerged early in the wake of the new modelling tools. In fact, it has become increasingly easy to achieve abstract sketch designs (surfaces) that satisfy these terms and thereby achieve the measure of elegance defined here. However, surface compositions are only the first sketchy step in the design of an elegant architecture.

Constructing Elegance

The next obvious challenge is to go beyond pure surfaces and to elaborate structural systems that are compatible with this ambition for continuous differentiation, perhaps even enhancing the overall effect of integrated complexity. One of

the most convincing contributions is Jesse Reiser's notion of a 'space-frame' exemplified in his competition entry for Manhattan's West Side in 1999.[9] In the work of Reiser + Umemoto, the space-frame becomes a space-filling medium that could receive continuous deformations that inform the system by allowing disturbances (squeezes, clearances, inserted objects) to radiate through the space-frame.

The next step was the focus on the envelope: how to tessellate or panelise continuously changing double-curved surfaces and, further, how to integrate (rather than merely impose) openings.

Naturally, on the way to the elaboration of fully functional, fully detailed designs, whereby more systems or layers need to be integrated, the principle of inflection (organic inter-articulation) becomes even more difficult to maintain. And in addition, the visual field is in danger of being overcrowded, compromising legibility and orientation.

It is at this moment of mounting difficulty – in the face of bringing the new paradigm into large-scale realisation – that elegance becomes an explicit priority, not least because the built results have all too often been disappointing in this respect. Already on the level of detailed digital modelling, every new layer of function or detailing requires a new,

Exterior cone. The lateral openings are of two kinds: the large openings are conic sections that produce the characteristic paraboloid form, and the smaller openings come in swarms that are articulated as variations of the swarm of voids that make up the waffle slab.

increasing ingenuity to be (seamlessly) incorporated. With a view to execution, further demands of geometric lawfulness, precision and high-order surface continuity become paramount concerns. Contemporary car design affords a challenging benchmark both in terms of the tight inflective nesting of multiple functional features and in terms of surface continuity. The obvious progress of the last few years is equally reliant upon digital design and manufacturing. For example, observe the way the headlights of the latest Mercedes sports cars are massaged into the subtle surface of the chassis.

Criteria and Postulates of Elegance

The notion of elegance promoted here still gives a certain relevance to Leon Battista Alberti's criterion of beauty: you can neither add nor subtract without destroying the harmony achieved. Except in the case of contemporary elegance, the overall composition lacks this sense of perfect closure that is implied in Alberti's conception. Alberti focused on key ordering principles, such as symmetry and proportion, which were seen as integrating the various parts into a whole by means of setting the parts into definite relations of relative position and proportion in analogy to the human figure. Perhaps the best example of this ideal is the Palladian villa. In

contrast, contemporary projects remain incomplete compositions, more akin to the Deleuzian notion of assemblage than to the classical conception of the organism. Our current idea of organic integration does not rely on fixed ideal types. Neither does it presuppose any proportional system, nor does it privilege symmetry. Instead, the parts or subsystems mutually inflect and adapt to each other, achieving integration via various modes of spatial interlocking, soft transitions at the boundaries between parts, morphological affiliation and so on.

Thus the principle of elegance postulates: do not add or subtract without elaborate inflections, mediations or inter-articulations.

While the classical concept of preordained perfection has been abandoned, there remains a strong sense of increasing tightness and stringency, even approaching a sense of internal necessity, as the network of compositional relations is elaborated and tightened. The more the compositional cross-referencing, inflection and organic inter-articulation within the design has been advanced, the harder it becomes to add or subtract elements. This kind of design trajectory, although wide open at the beginning, beyond a certain point becomes heavily self-constraining. One might be inclined to talk about

Each cone has its own variation of angles and radii that blend seamlessly into the waffle slab above. The cones also re-emerge within the interior, either as craters or as cones that continue to carry the space-frame above. There is an essential symbiosis in the spatial and structural conception of the building, and a close inter-articulation of the waffle concrete structure of the raised floor and the steel space-frame that carries the roof.

the increasing self-determination of a composition: an emergent (rather than preordained) perfection.

The systems theorist Niklas Luhmann has emphasised this phenomenon, which he has termed the 'self-programming'[10] of the individual artwork that might be observed within all artistic work that is concerned with the elaboration of complex artefacts, whether elaborate paintings, musical compositions or literary works. Luhmann takes account of 'the necessity that manifests itself in the artwork'. He elaborates: 'In this sense, creating a work of art … generates the freedom to make decisions on the basis of which one can continue one's work. The freedoms and necessities one encounters are entirely … consequences of decisions made within the work. The necessity of certain consequences one experiences in one's work … is not imposed … but results from the fact that one began, and how. This entails the risk of running into insoluble problems …'[11]

Designers know how a design trajectory can lead into a dead end, can fail to 'work' or remain unresolved. The elegance we refer to – elegance on top of complexity – is a tall order and cannot be secured in advance. Although we can provide certain recipes, such as the employment of global distortions to cohere a field of fragments, the result cannot be guaranteed.

With increasing complexity, the maintenance of elegance becomes increasingly demanding.

Complexity and elegance stand in a relation of precarious mutual amplification: a relation of increasingly improbable mutual enhancement; that is, mutual amplification with increasing probability of collapse.

Arguing for Elegance

Why should we bother to strive for this increasingly difficult elegance? Does it serve a purpose beyond itself?

The overriding headline here is: 'Orientation within complex organisations.' Contemporary architectural briefs are marked by a demand for more complex and simultaneous programmatic provisions to be organised within more complex urban contexts. Elegance allows for an increased programmatic complexity to coincide with a relative reduction of visual complication by means of integrating multiple elements into a coherent and continuous formal and spatial system. The general challenge is to find modes of composition that can articulate complex arrangements and relationships without losing legibility and the capacity to orient users.

Elegance as defined here signifies this capacity to articulate complex life-processes in a way that can maintain overall comprehension, legibility and continuous orientation within the composition. In this vein, Zaha Hadid Architects has been promoting an architecture without corners, because corners pollute the visual field usually without signifying anything (unless they are specifically made to signify something).

Complex organisational relations of overlapping or interpenetrating domains can be articulated and made legible so that a complex order is perceived rather than allowing the complexity to appear as disorder. The user might, for example,

Every cone acts as both structural element and programmatic effect.

be able to perceive his or her position as one where several domains intersect or (more ambitious) where multiple perspectives unravel the spatial interpenetration of multiple simultaneous use-patterns relating to the multiple audiences that tend to coincide in contemporary institutions. But how can this be achieved?

Traditionally, spatial orientation has been operating primarily on the basis of relations of inclusion or containment – the Russian doll principle of nesting domains. Spatial position is defined as a series of relations of containments: continent, country, region, city, district, neighbourhood, estate, building, floor, apartment, room. Each domain has a clear boundary and is fully contained within a larger domain with an equally crisp boundary. This is how one knows where one is at any time. A change of position implies the crossing of a boundary. Orientation is traditionally further supported if the domains can be identified with easily recognisable platonic/geometric figures such as circles, squares or rectangles. Domains and figures are ideally kept separate. It should be obvious that the scope of this system of ordering is limited. A sense of order can only be maintained on the basis of a radical reductionism that is antithetical to the realities of contemporary life. On the one hand this predicament leads to the fallacy of minimalism craving for an artificial simplicity, and on the other to the fetishistic embrace of disorder, as in the celebration of Tokyo's visual chaos.

A radically different, alternative mode of ordering and orientation is afforded by the principles of elegance discussed above. Here, figures and domains need not sustain platonic simplicity because their deformation no longer spells the break down of order, but the lawful inscription of information. Figures/domains do not have to remain neatly separated because we have developed lawful rules of mutual inflection, and lawful rules of gradual transformation.

Orientation in a complex, lawfully differentiated field affords navigation along vectors of transformation – for example, a morphing trajectory – rather than snapping from position to position via boundary crossings. In the extreme case of a pure field condition, both bounded domains and identifiable figures have in fact disappeared and orientation along reference objects and bounded/nested domains is fully replaced by the navigation of lawfully modulated field qualities such as density, directionality, agitation in the field and so on, affording inferences and anticipations. ∆

Notes

1. The concept of *Abstract Machine* has been imported from Deleuze and Guattari *A Thousand Plateaus*. Within architectural discourse the concept denotes open-ended design processes that submit to runaway graphic or computational processes, thus suspending purpose and rational control. Eisenman's formal transformational series has been a seminal precursor.
2. At this juncture the protagonists involved typically bifurcate into two distinct groups with two quite different career trajectories: those who go mainstream together with the innovations they contributed to, and those who stay within the domain of the avant-garde to move on into further unknown territory.
3. The elaboration of a descriptive language is a precondition for any theory and an extremely important mechanism for directed architectural creativity. However, it is this second, argumentative component that can sustain the claim for the pertinence of the trend pushed here.
4. The avoidance of the loaded concept of beauty and its attendant disputes does not exclude the recognition that there are certain (perhaps inevitable) continuities with certain prior reflections around the concept of beauty. In fact this emphasis on establishing coherence within the differentiated – unity in difference – is reminiscent of Francis Hutcheson's notion of beauty as a 'compound ratio of uniformity and variety'. See Francis Hutcheson, *Inquiry into the Original of Our Ideas of Beauty and Virtue*, London, 1725, critical edition The Hague, 1973, p 38. Also see Hogarth's notion of 'composed variety' in William Hogarth, *The Analysis of Beauty*, Yale University Press (New Haven and London), 1997, p 28. My emphasis on ordered complexity might be understood as a radicalisation of Hogarth's notion of 'composed variety'. Hogarth, theorising the aesthetics of the Rococo, is promoting variety against sameness, but insists on composed variety 'for variety uncomposed, and without design, is confusion and deformity' (p 28).
5. What Frei Otto called 'formfinding', Lars Spuybroek refers to as 'material computing' in order to emphasise the similarity of those physical processes with the by now familiar and ubiquitous digital-modelling techniques offered by animation software such as Maya.
6. Robert Venturi, *Complexity and Contradiction in Architecture*, 2nd edn, Museum of Modern Art (New York), 1977, p 88.
7. Ibid, p 89.
8. For instance, Bernard Tschumi's Parc de la Villette, in contrast, still operates with layers that remain indifferent to each other. The introduction of inflection marks the shift from Deconstructivism to folding.
9. 'West Side Convergence Competition Entry, New York 1999', in Reiser + Umemoto, *Atlas of Novel Tectonics*, Princeton Architectural Press (New York), 2006, p 128.
10. Niklas Luhmann, *Art as Social System*, Stanford University Press (Stanford, CA), 2000, p 204.
11. Ibid, pp 203–4.

These regulations structure a repertoire of operations that allow for the adaptable handling of all sorts of functional and contextual contingencies without losing formal consistency. Such a regulated repertoire of design moves is the precondition (not the guarantee) of elegance. More universal rules like balancing within an asymmetric, dynamic equilibrium, and a certain (new, stretched) range of plausible proportions are still to be observed. Both concerns (dynamic equilibrium and proportion) also pertain to the rhythmic flow of the interior spaces.

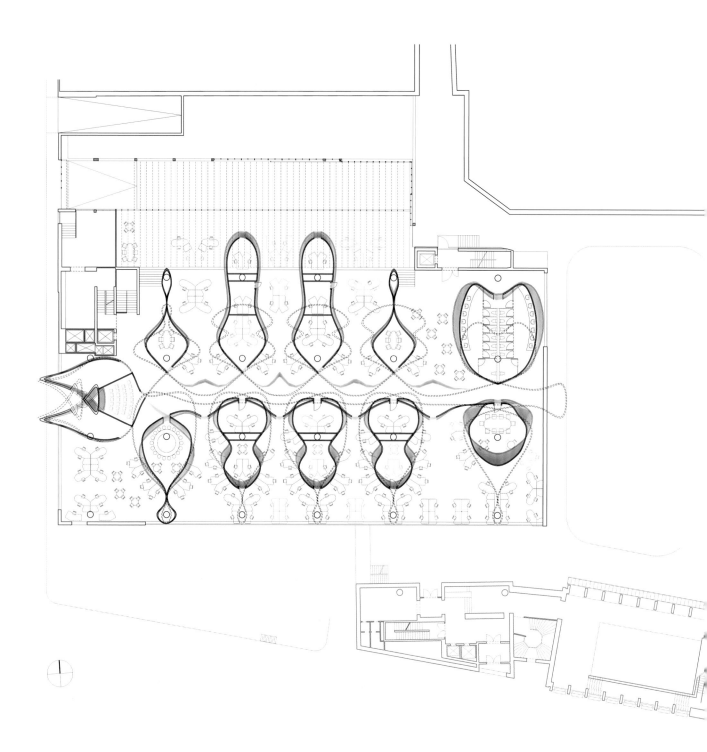

Surface Continuity

An Elegant Integration

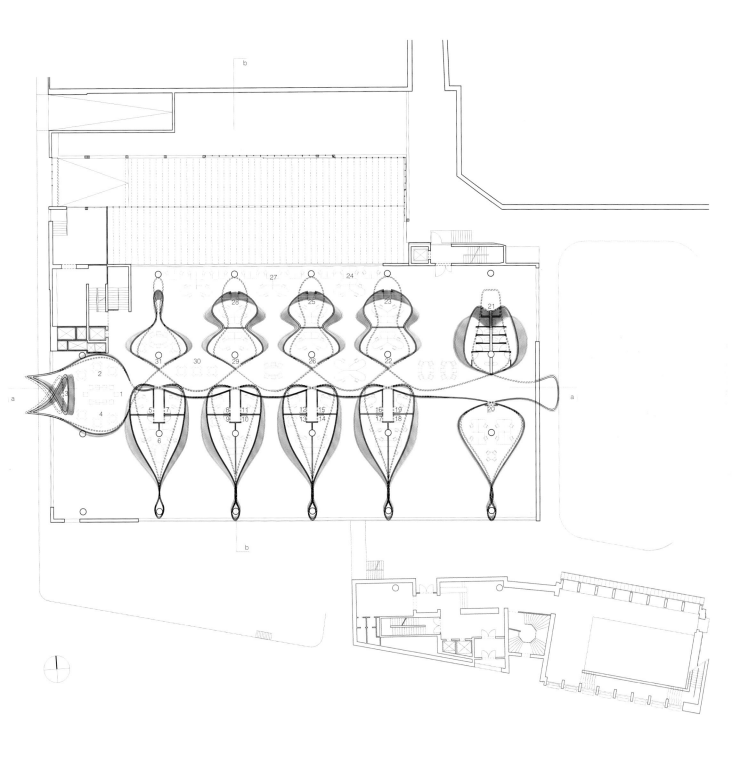

Greg Lynn FORM, DADAGROWS, Florence, Italy, 2001
The interior landscape rejects the typically gridded uniform pattern of office cubicles in favour of work-group gradient fields of organic office bundles. The curvaceous interior partitions allow for a spatial flow that enhances cooperation, communication and creativity within the company and its various divisions.

Elegance in architecture owes much to a finely honed calibration of scale. Ali Rahim and Hina Jamelle describe how Greg Lynn FORM's designs for the DADA SpA competition in Florence and the BMW Leipzig Factory express a sophisticated understanding of the relationship of individual parts to the whole. In both projects, a carefully modulated family of interrelated parts anticipate future users' desire for spatial flexibility. The scale also allows for changes and transformations in surfaces' form. Smooth transitions are assured by material suppleness and enhanced by atmospheric artificial lighting.

Greg Lynn's designs articulate a very suggestive future for elegance. In both projects featured here there is an overwhelming interest in effortlessly tying together organisational, spatial and aesthetic features through continuity in surface and material to yield projects that develop in response to social interactivity and collaboration. The occurrence of these conditions is enabled by the inclusive nature and scale of the part-to-whole relations of the forms that constitute the project interiors. Each interior is a family of forms that grows in complexity as the forms are hybridised, producing a continuity incorporative of differences, and generating a set of distinctive moods for the interior that are further enhanced by the orchestration of lighting effects.

The transformation of the organisational diagram provides a new alternative to existing organisational structures. Transformation is achieved through a critical siting of spaces, entries and vertical circulation for workers and services in such a manner as to create new spatial organisation figures for buildings. For example, the design for the BMW Leipzig Factory presented the challenge of creating a flexible office space and factory environment through which partially assembled motor vehicles would be transported. Lynn responded by designing the space as a high-performance machine, spatially centred around the functional aspects of the programme, including inspection, quality assurance, research, measurement and visualisation. For DADAGROWS, the interior landscape rejects the typical uniform grid pattern of office cubicles and instead introduces work-group-based gradient fields. Organic office bundles allow the space to be loosely organised as fields of work and relaxation punctuated by nodes of communication and interaction, as well as nodes of supervision and administration.

In both projects, spatiality is transformed by the fluidity of a continuous surface that gradually rises from the ground, comprising a family of interrelated forms. The transformation between the forms, the relations between parts and the whole, and the scale of their transformation affords the possibility of modulating the spatial atmosphere within the projects. Since the forms bear a family relation, this allows for the integration and separation of very particular dimensions of each form in response to specific uses, and also for the

precise modulation of each form's curvature in order to produce gradients of interaction. In the BMW project, the spaces encapsulated by the forms weave a continuity between the architecture and the automobile, and allow for social and technical synergy between three programmatically disparate parts of the plant. In DADAGROWS, there is a coherent continuity to the interior surfaces of the entire complex, allowing for a smooth pedestrian flow that enhances cooperation, communication and creativity within the company and its various divisions, though each space simultaneously retains its own unique identity.

The complex formal relationships that are provided in these designs yield a range of moods that are further enhanced by the careful modulation of direct and indirect light to complement the fluidity of the forms. Multiple effects result from light falling on the curved surfaces, allowing for the spaces to evoke different moods and emotions depending on material finishes and the location of users relative to each surface. For BMW, the volumes are treated with a metallic paint and lit by a system of skylights running through the building in a linear manner. Daylight bounces off these metallic surfaces, eliminating the glare associated with direct sunlight and resulting in a diffused light for the offices and factory. Simultaneously, this produces the aesthetic effect of bathing special functions in natural daylight and accentuating the highlights and curvature of the enclosure itself. In DADAGROWS, the interiors include a diversity of surface materials, luminous effects and spatial forms, highlighting the submersive qualities of the spaces.

Elegance in Lynn's work is contained in the organisational, spatial and aesthetic fluidity of his projects. Each of these criteria is designed to individually create a particular sensibility, but elegance ultimately resides in the seamless integration of all these factors as they are brought together in a single, sinuous form. Distinguished by being inclusive, yet precise, this form integrates all the complexities of architecture in one continuously transforming project. The moods and atmospheres generated within the work belie a sense of elegance that is greater than the sum of its component parts.

Project description provided by Greg Lynn **FORM**

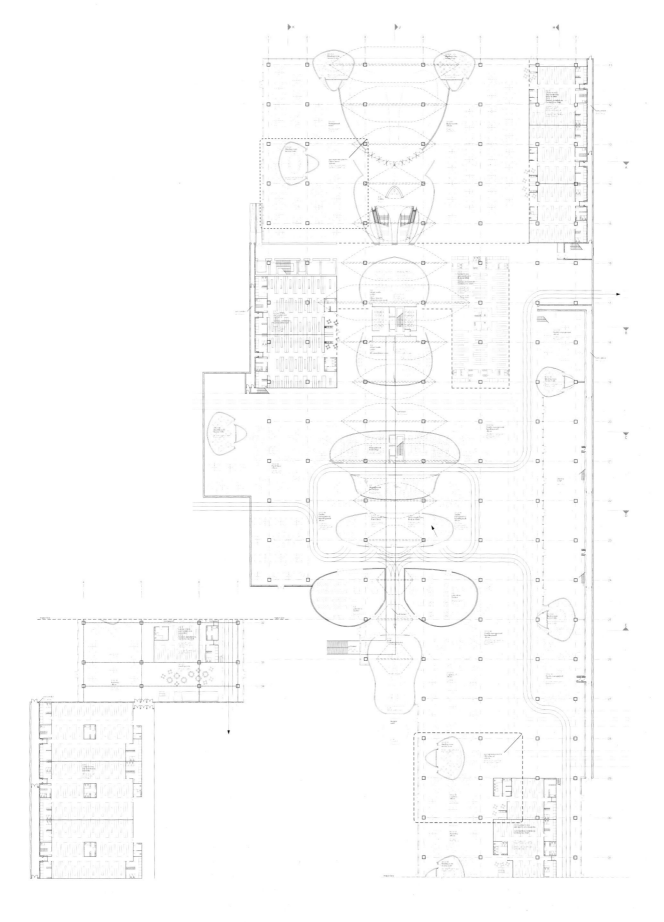

Greg Lynn FORM, BMW Leipzig Factory, Leipzig, Germany, 2002
The guiding principle of the design is that the spatial, social and aesthetic features of the space derive from the
technical and functional organisation of the central building.

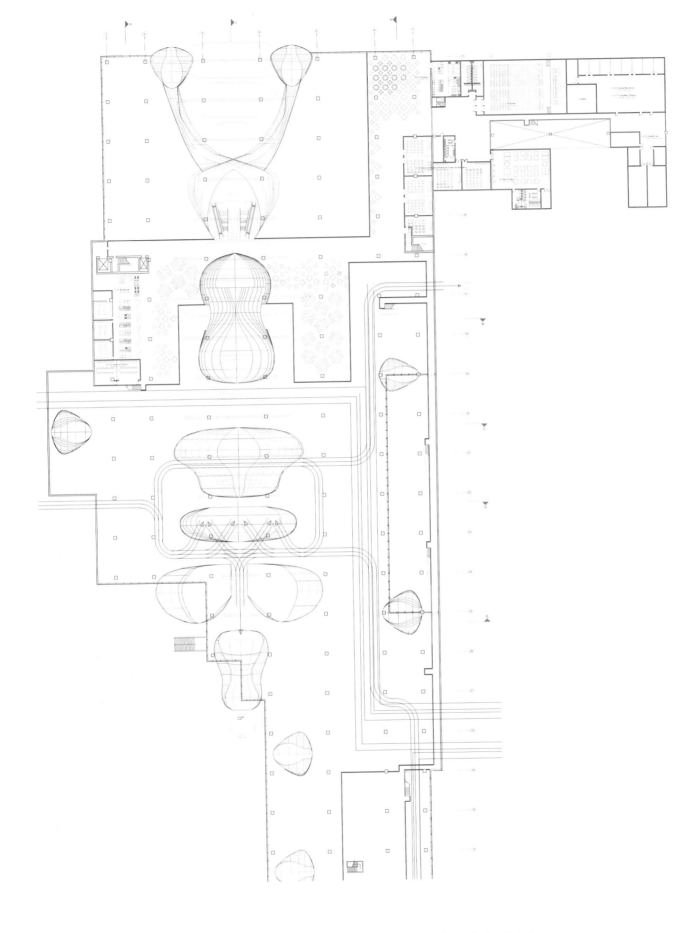

The metallic volumes eliminate glare and direct sunlight in the offices and factory and also have the aesthetic effect of bathing the special functions in natural daylight and accentuating the highlights and curvature of their enclosure.

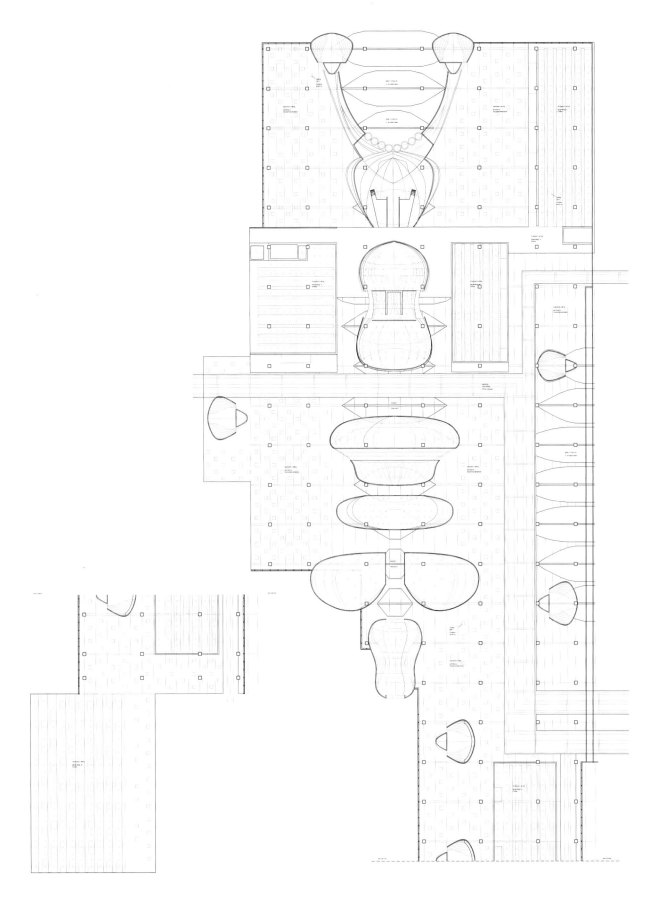

The complex formal relationships yield a range of moods enhanced by the careful modulation of both direct and indirect light and atmospheric artificial light. ∆

Everything is Curved

The Mercedes-Benz Museum, Stuttgart, Germany

In the Mercedez-Benz Museum, Stuttgart, organisational and spatial strategies combine to yield an elegant form. Its presence, formal balance and refinement of features, along with its continuity of surface, create a building that is spatially and formally opulent. The structure rises above its context, while achieving harmony through its spatial configuration, which defies gravity – cars and people are able to drive and walk up the building. **Ben van Berkel** and **Caroline Bos** of UNStudio describe here how they set out to achieve this by dedicating the spatiotemporal experience of the museum to motion and reiteration.

Everything that a museum generally is, the Mercedes-Benz Museum is not. There are no oversized yet confined spaces (are they corridors or are they rooms?) in which time stands oppressively still and even the most alert visitor quickly succumbs to stupor. There are no walls of unrelenting uniformity and blankness that absorb the art that hangs on them, rendering it equally uniform and blank. In a sense, there are no walls; there are no rooms (and there is no art, or is there?). The spatiotemporal experience is dedicated to movement and is felt throughout. The visitor scrolls through the building as if moving through a time machine. History begins at the top and recedes along the way down, ending with the future.

This sense of sequence is amplified by structural repetitions and the curvilinear geometry of the building with its trefoil organisation. The geometry of the plan, with its three overlapping circles, is suggestive of a trajectory subject to centrifugal forces which propel the visitor around. The trefoil is a variation of the same mathematical model belonging to the field of knot theory on which the Möbius strip and its three-dimensional variant, the Klein Bottle, are based. As a model it suggests the infrastructure of architecture, the way in which a building can be constructed according to how one moves through it. The trefoil possesses topological qualities: movement, orientation and direction are

---

UNStudio, Mercedes-Benz Museum, Stuttgart, Germany, 2006
Previous spread: The success of a museum structure depends on the inventiveness and adequacy of its internal arrangement of spaces. The art of the Mercedes-Benz Museum is that it binds together several radical spatial principles and generates a new typology as a result.
Right: The effect of free, unobstructed spaces flowing into each other is the result of the museum's intricate load-bearing construction. This construction system, in turn, is integrated with the circulation system, which takes up and transforms the challenging structure.

The focus is on the oblique as a means to stimulate mobility, sense of direction and communication.

intrinsic to its structure. Within it the visitor is always located at some point on a curve, thus there are no abrupt transitions, no discontinuities. The space (the time) the visitor leaves behind is undividedly part of the space the individual is in now, is part of his or her ecological field, still perceptible, still surrounding the visitor as if following him or her.

This sensation of being followed by space is a new type of experience. We wonder: why don't architects today experiment more with space-enhancing techniques? For centuries perspective has been used as a tool to stimulate perception, but perspectival distortion represents just one technique to enrich awareness of space. Curved spaces go much further than extending the forward-looking gaze; they open up a polycentric, camera-like perception of space into all directions and dimensions. Curved, continuous space with its diagonal transecting spaces delivers unexpected sensations of spatiality. Orientation is almost impossible, although it is equally impossible to lose one's way. Stacking several trefoils on top each other, rotating the petals and alternating between single- and double-height floors has resulted in solid, curving masses of concrete that embrace voids and steer the gaze in all directions, except straight ahead.

The oblique condition is ideal for the museum as it brings into being spaces that provide minimum distraction. The repetition of oblique elements is combined with another architectural ingredient: the curve.

The use of angles in walls, floors and ceilings gives the eye something to focus on, and the repetition of these elements paradoxically results in environments that are experienced as tranquil.

The Mercedes-Benz Museum is a building of curves and repetitions. The mathematical model of the trefoil, again like the Möbius strip, encompasses the themes of the combinatorial and the serial. Organising space in a sequence of sets, like serial music does with notes, is also something that is underexplored in contemporary architecture, where the notion of repetition is misunderstood. It is confused with the Modernist principle of standardization – the breakdown of

architecture into mass-produced elements. Repetition in architecture is seen as a matter of economic expediency, rather than of genuine interest or experiment, and is associated more with production processes than design processes.

Yet from the point of view of both the production (but in this case design production rather than the process of building) and reception of architecture, the theme of repetition can, and needs to be, thought and worked

Folding surfaces are produced by the fusion of curvature and obliqueness.

The fold, usually incarnated in a very visible way, here becomes invisible under a self-imposed regime of inclusiveness.

A structure-giving system and a daylight-bringing device were absorbed into the building's construction, facilitating the separation and rejoining of the two different types of exhibition spaces.

through much more fully. Repetition endows themes with longevity. Retracing one's steps, doing the same thing again, but differently this time, is a form of consistency without which architecture would not be possible – there would be no habitable space.

Repetitions generate an aggregate with densifications, intensifications and intervals. Repetition brings sonority. It allows for improvisation, it marks territory, it codes milieus. The Mercedes-Benz Museum is a space-time consolidation with two marked rhythms: the stories of collections and myths cascading down and bound together by a double helix. Its structural and curvilinear repetitions produce a museum without rooms, without walls, and without art (or do they?). **∆**

The plans and facades merge oblique surfaces with symmetrical curves, engendering deep, asymmetrical spaces.

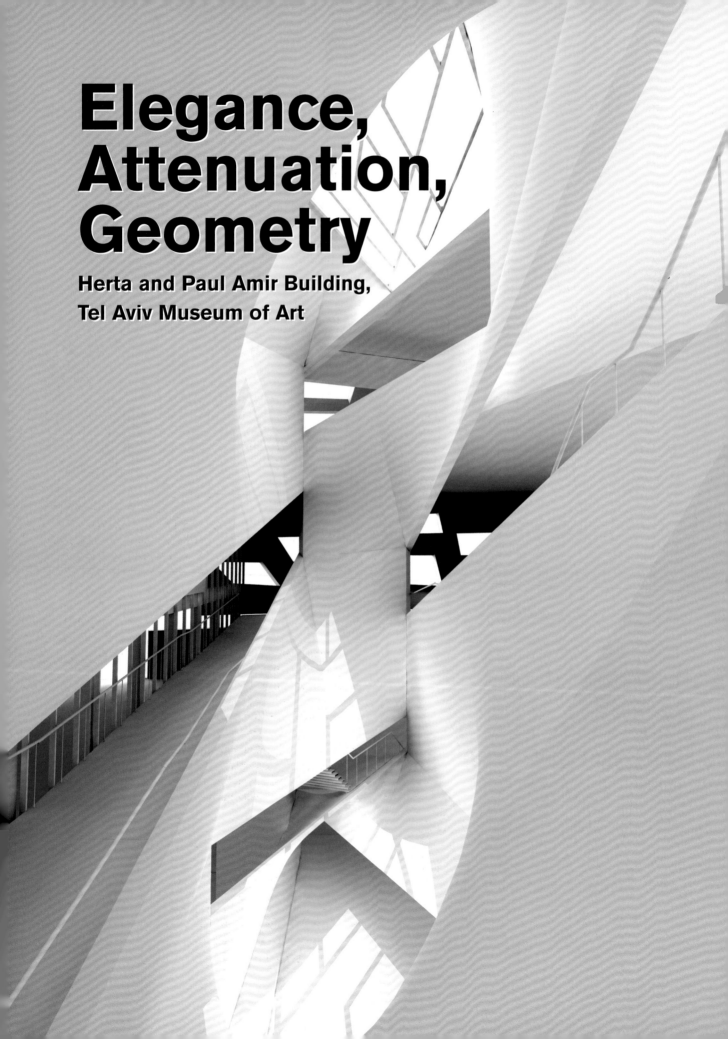

Elegance, Attenuation, Geometry

Herta and Paul Amir Building,
Tel Aviv Museum of Art

Preston Scott Cohen explores the elegant through the eye of projective geometry. He finds 'fruitful lessons' in the architecture of the Baroque, which offers a historical model of anamorphosis (the extreme perspectival condition in which an image appears distorted) and tectonic distortion.

Broadly speaking, architecture can be considered to be elegant when it is restrained, refined and precise. But the constituents of elegance that lend themselves most readily to the production of architecture are much narrower in scope. In particular, these include the slender proportions that result from attenuation.

Attenuation exemplifies a paradox inscribed within both elegance and architecture. Both are defined as much by objective criteria as by subjective experience. Elegance aims to reconcile the momentary and the eternal, whereas style is a time-bound category. Elegance thus stands in contrast to the passing of time that is measured by the stylish and the fashionable. Yet, while its reference to a condition that ostensibly operates outside of time recalls the classical appeal to permanent values, the effects with which elegance are most immediately associated are contingent and temporal, and thus quintessentially modern.

Attenuated proportions are one of several manifestations of elasticity, the dynamic and continuous adjustment of proportions that in contemporary architecture is defined by

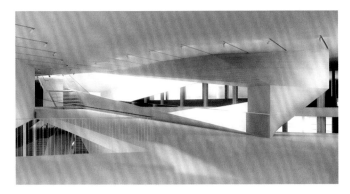

Preston Scott Cohen, Herta and Paul Amir Building, Tel Aviv Museum of Art, Israel, 2003–09
Above: Lobby view. The implicitly kinetic figures of the exterior volume and the interior 'lightfall' at once determine, and are determined by, the disparate angles between the rectangular galleries and the angled site boundaries. Extending towards the sky, the parabolas of the lightfall guide visitors into the architecture galleries, Israeli art galleries, auditorium, library, special exhibitions and other programmes.
Opposite: View of the central atrium. Located in the centre of the city's cultural complex, the Tel Aviv Museum of Art poses an extraordinary architectural challenge, one that bears directly on the motion/stasis duality of elegance: how to resolve the tension between a tight, idiosyncratic triangular site and the museum's need for a series of large, neutral rectangular galleries. The Herta and Paul Amir Building extension to the museum introduces subtly twisting geometric forms, based on hyperbolic parabolas, that unify the galleries with their context and simultaneously bring natural light into its deepest recesses.

parametric equations, those based upon mathematical constraints, nowadays digitally mediated. The roots of proportional elasticity are grounded in projective geometry, which of all the geometries used in architecture is the most susceptible to engagement with the circumstantial aspects of architectural production and reception.

Applied to architecture, projective geometry is capable of mediating the absolute and the contingent, the universal and the particular, the part and the whole. Perhaps this is due to the fact that the 17th-century method was, from its inception, impure. It was developed for the purpose of being applied to other fields of knowledge, such as fortifications, topographic mapping and naval engineering. The most instrumental ties between projective geometry and architecture were established for the purpose of representation and masonry construction by means of perspective and stereotomy.

Two parallel developments in Baroque architecture offer fruitful lessons on the possible use of projective geometry as an instrument of mediation with particular relevance to the possibility of a paradoxical foundation for a Modern architecture: anamorphosis and tectonic distortion. Both are paradoxical as foundations because they involve deviations rather than rules; both have the additional property of embedding geometrical characteristics within the perceptual and material circumstances of buildings. Anamorphosis is understood to be an extreme condition of perspective in which an image, or a part of an image, appears to be distorted from a frontal view and must be viewed from an extreme oblique position to be seen undistorted. Like the attenuated condition that would seem to be an essential attribute of elegance, anamorphosis involves a deviation from the rule which calls attention to that rule.

It has been argued that its antecedent, Albertian perspective, aspired to establish a metrical reciprocity in which perspective, the centralised plan governed by the grid of architecture, and the observer are unified. With anamorphosis, this unity is torn asunder. Anamorphosis divides in two the pictorial space of representation, then distorts one and superimposes it on the other demanding the observer move between frontal and oblique positions. In so far as perspective is divided, the observer is disassociated from it. The movement between poles is something like an attenuated space. All of this takes place within a very specific context of iconological codes and political matrices in which secret meanings are disclosed only to those who can read the anamorphic code.

In the architectural tectonics of the Baroque, one episode of particular interest to this analysis stands out. There are certain 17th-century facades in Milan, Rome and Turin that, insofar as they are curved, reunify all of the elements of the classical tectonic system according to a nonclassical paradigm of order. The classical intricacy of parts and proportional relationships is manifest anew in a singular, elastic form. Here we are confronted by an objective dynamism akin to the perceptual dynamism of anamorphosis.

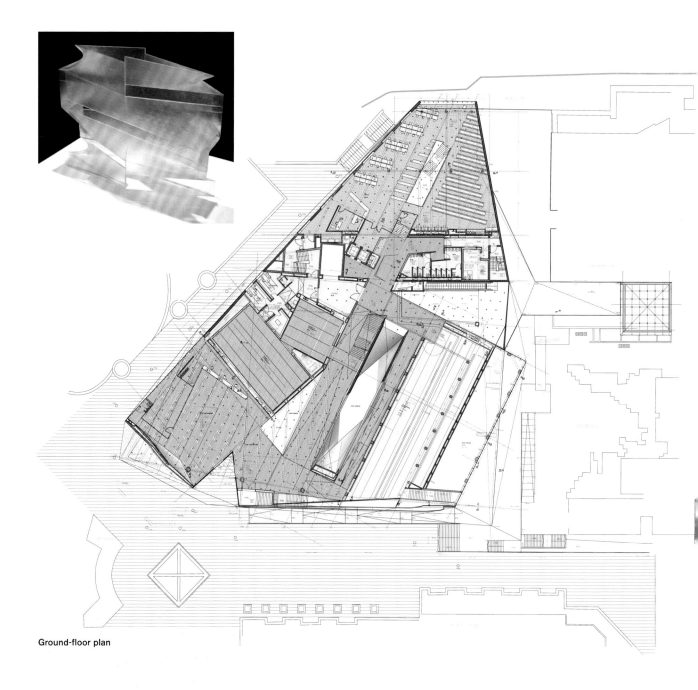

Ground-floor plan

To a certain extent, the Baroque is the nearest approximation of anamorphosis in architecture. It can be summarised as a battle between firmitas and plasticity. To make an obvious distinction, unlike its architectural counterpart, anamorphosis makes its discordance explicit. But, the Baroque synthesis also involves the superimposition of two antithetical conditions – motion and stasis – in a single instance just as anamorphosis did with distortion and correction. And whereas in anamorphosis the resolution of incompatible representations unfolds temporally, in the Baroque the divergent representations are simultaneous. In this regard, the Baroque denies temporality even as the idea of motion as a temporal category is retained.

With anamorphosis and Baroque curvature, the unity of the subject with perspectival and gridded architectural space is replaced by a new subjectivity, one in which the subject, viewing from the oblique, becomes a spectator of elastic transformations. This spectator observes an oscillation between norms and extremes. The elasticity that results from this oscillation establishes a modern, disenchanted subject far from the static and harmonic unity of objects and subjects hypothesised by the classical. From this standpoint, we can understand that the Baroque is like a freezing of motion, an unclassical stasis. From the standpoint of the preceding discussion, one can say that the anamorphic (which entails time-bound motion) and the Baroque (which entails frozen motion, motion eternalised) establish significant parallels to the temporality of elegance that lies between the two poles.

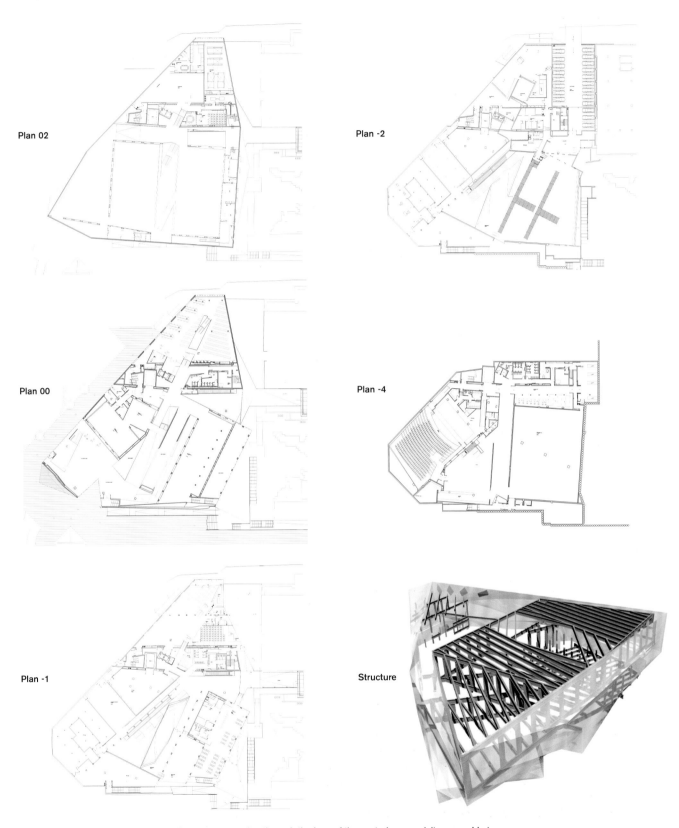

Plan 02

Plan -2

Plan 00

Plan -4

Plan -1

Structure

Walking from gallery to gallery inside the museum, gazing through the lens of the central space, visitors are able to discern relationships among all interior and exterior spaces. The building is composed according to multiple axes that deviate significantly from floor to floor. In essence, it is a series of independent plans stacked one atop the other, connected by geometrically articulated episodes of vertical circulation. The steel structural system is stacked accordingly, its members navigating the many subtle level changes necessitated by the site and resolved by the ramps and stairs. Cantilevers allow the discrepancies between the plans and provide overhangs at the perimeter of the building.

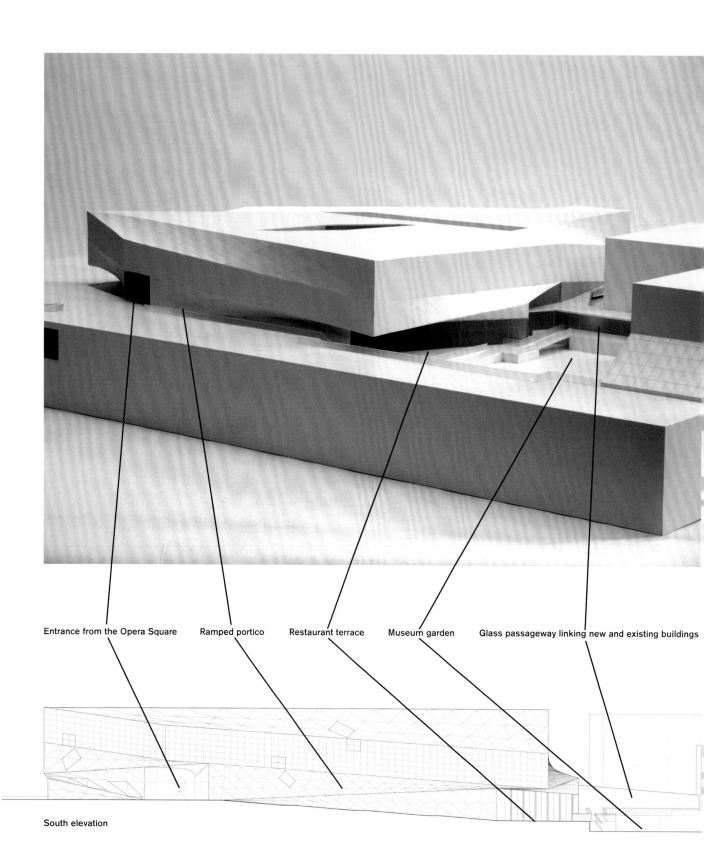

Entrance from the Opera Square   Ramped portico   Restaurant terrace   Museum garden   Glass passageway linking new and existing buildings

South elevation

The parabolas of the facade are panellised into four sided plane surfaces, able to be varied and adjusted parametrically to allow for deviations that will inevitably emerge during construction. The panels are subdivided into stone pieces no heavier than 60 kilograms (132 pounds), thus enabling assembly from a scaffold instead of lifting by cranes and contending with eccentric angles of loading due to the constantly varying shapes.

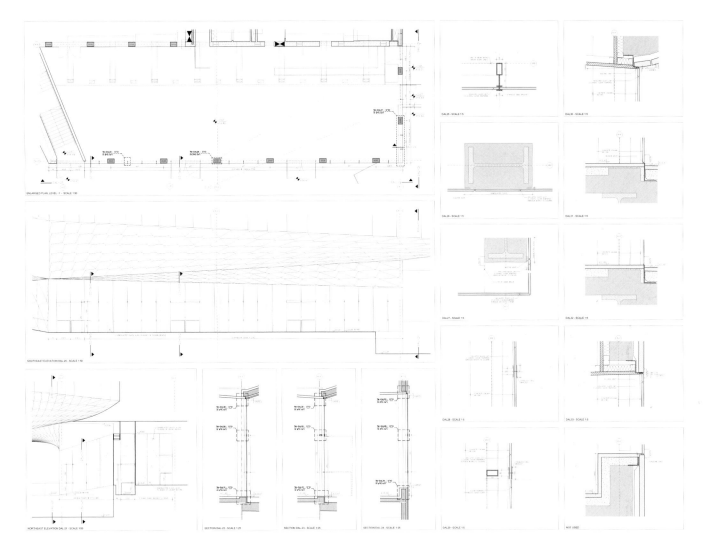

East elevation details

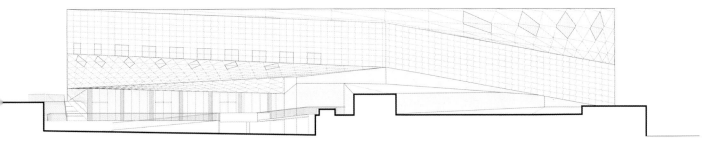

East elevation

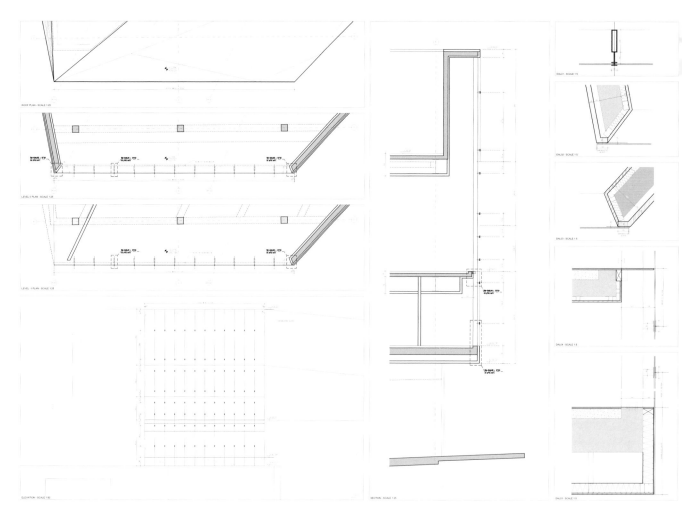

Details of library window

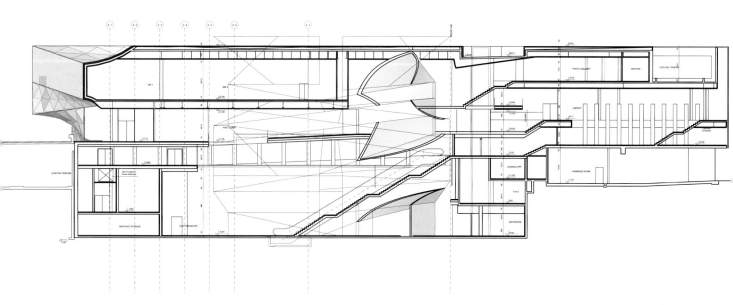

North–South section

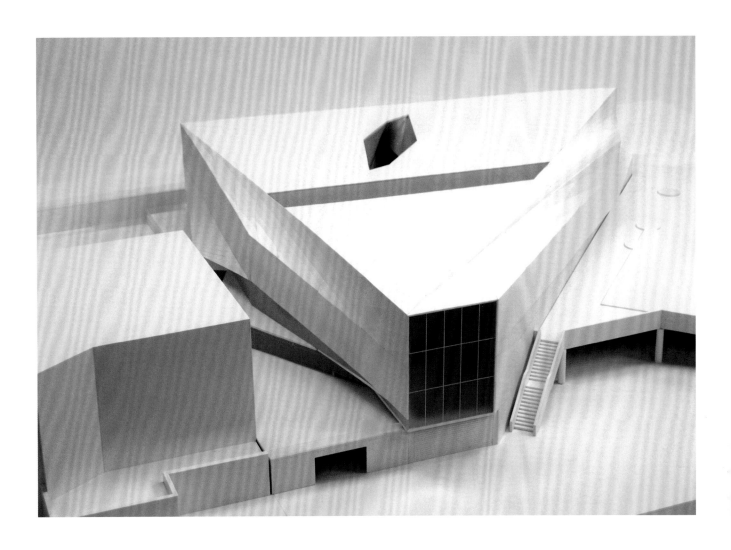

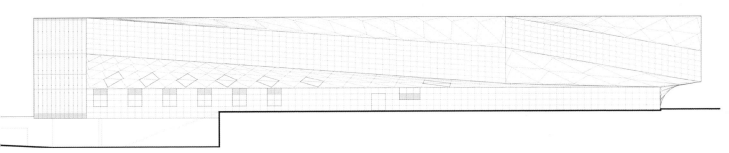

West elevation

Construction details. The quad panelised facade thus serves as a rain-screen cladding the roughly parabolic structural concrete wall behind. The stone, though indigenous, gives shape to a synthetic whole that is nevertheless unprecedented in the city. It is accomplished by methods that become economically feasible by digital means. ⚿

Beyond the Structural Ski

ha Hadid Architects: Marsa Dubai Residential T

Continuity of surface and structure when combined with a formal response to existing site-features deliver a potent elegance. Ali Rahim and **Hina Jamelle** describe how Zaha Hadid Architects in their Marsa Dubai Residential Tower were able to adapt the internal organisation to site constraints and the building's immediate environment. This renders a sophisticated aesthetic, which neither impacts external conditions nor compromises the interior spaces.

Zaha Hadid Architects' Marsa Dubai Residential Tower integrates structure and skin with a gradient of porosities that intensify as one ascends, creating differing atmospheres throughout the height of the project. This unifying continuity of structure and skin may at first seem to be the principle feature that lends this project elegance. But on closer examination it becomes apparent that elegance is ultimately made possible by the building's masterful use of technique to mediate a broader range of architectural and contextual complexities. In the tower, the structural and enclosure systems are interrelated to organisational, spatial and site issues to generate a legible formal strategy and set of aesthetic qualities that can ultimately be appreciated by the viewer as elegant.

Key to the project is an inventive structural system that is specifically integrated with the surface. The system consists of two vertical concrete tubes, one of which resides within the other. The interior tube contains circulation and core building services, while the outer tube forms the exterior skin of the

project, extending through the structure's height. The exterior skin is punctured with openings covering up to 40 per cent of its surface arranged to form a gradation from a few small openings at the tower's base to more frequent, larger openings at the top. As one moves upwards, there are also an increased number of geometrically faceted windows whose design draws from traditional Islamic motifs. The balance of openings to opaque surface is crucial for the project to maintain its elegance: if the skin is compromised, so is the structure and, as a result, so is the overall elegance of the building.

The exterior skin is supple in that it incorporates all of the organisational and spatial relations of the building. The interior floor plates split in a scissor-like action and seesaw up the height of the structure. A variety of spatial conditions are thus created to accommodate the building's diverse programmes, which include underground and above-ground parking, a swimming pool, health club and multi-use hall, one- to three-bedroom apartments, and four-bedroom and penthouse suites. Functionally, the seesawing form creates a greater perimeter area that allows an increased amount of daylight to penetrate into the circulation core while still providing for control over the solar intensity admitted to the occupied spaces. Excellent daylighting levels are thus achieved throughout, reducing reliance on artificial lighting.

Closely related to this diversity of interior spatial programmes is a series of exterior transformations that allow the building to respond to its site constraints. Situated within a densely populated enclave in Dubai, the building twists to enjoy diagonal views of the Persian Gulf to the northeast and the marina to the southwest. Generated from a closed square plan, the tower is open at ground level on the south side to allow for public pedestrian access from the marina, while on the north side the inverse applies and the building splits open at its top to provide penthouse residents with spectacular views of the gulf.

External climactic conditions are mediated by variations within the building skin. The incorporation of a gradated range of openings, adjusted to the orientation of each facade, minimises the heat load within the building. On elevations most directly exposed to solar intensity, the glazing is recessed to maximise solar shading, while on other, less exposed elevations, it is positioned closer to the outside edge of the facade. Beyond providing environmental control, this adjustment of glazing position within the depth of the facade visually accentuates the building's changing shape and form. Tectonic inflection at this scale enhances its overall visual interest and at the same time contains variations within the range of a unifying appearance.

The Marsa Dubai Residential Tower houses an exuberant diversity of atmospheres and programmatic conditions within an overall form that integrates organisational, spatial, structural, surface and contextual conditions. The expertise in technique here allows for the seemingly effortless containment and incorporation of multiple architecture complexities, resulting in a form whose every surface exudes elegance.

Project information provided by Zaha Hadid Architects

Zaha Hadid Architects, Marsa Dubai Residential Tower, Dubai, United Arab Emirates, 2005
Above: The tower is one of two buildings on each side of the creek and the bridge crossing to the Jumeirah Beach Marina from the mainland that can be perceived as holding 'sentinel' positions in relation to the general masterplan and the growing number of buildings around the marina.
Opposite: From its prominent corner position at the eastern end of the marina, residents of the proposed tower will enjoy unparalleled diagonal views both outwards (northeast) to the gulf and inwards (southwest) towards the marina.

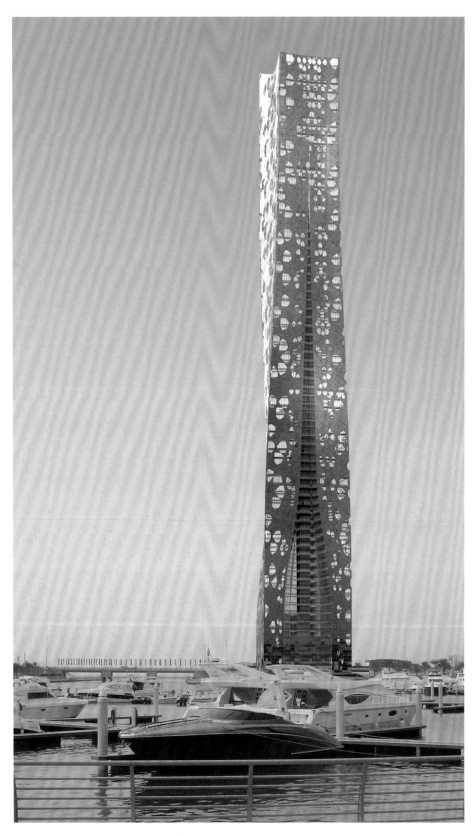

Left: Fenestration variation.
Right: The outer structural tube that is the facade can be punctuated by up to 40 per cent provided there is a gradation in the number and type of openings from few and small at the base to more and larger at the top. Thus the upwards gradation of the window pattern – designs that are drawn from studies of a traditional decorative faceted Islamic geometry.

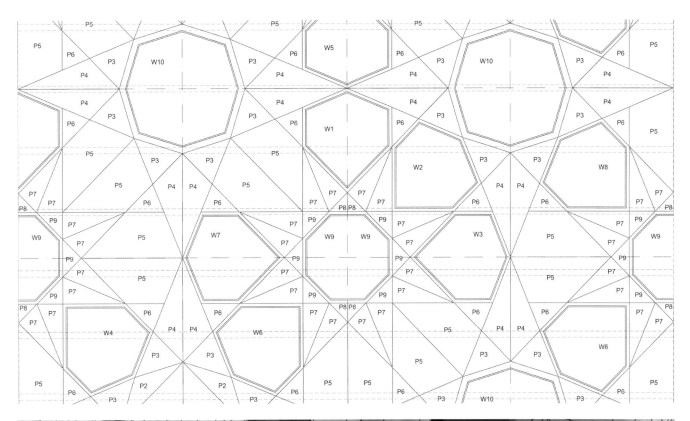

Top: The treatment of each facade is tailored to the particular elevation by varying the position of the glazing within the overall facade depth.
Bottom: Programmatically, four floors of parking are situated above the mezzanine floor levels, with three levels of parking underground. Commercial and civic programming is planned for the fifth and sixth floors, including shops, a swimming pool, health spa, gym, multi-use hall and kitchens. Above this public area, the remaining height of the tower is divided into two zones. In the lower half are 30 floors of one-, two- and three-bedroom apartments and duplexes arranged around a central service core. ⌂

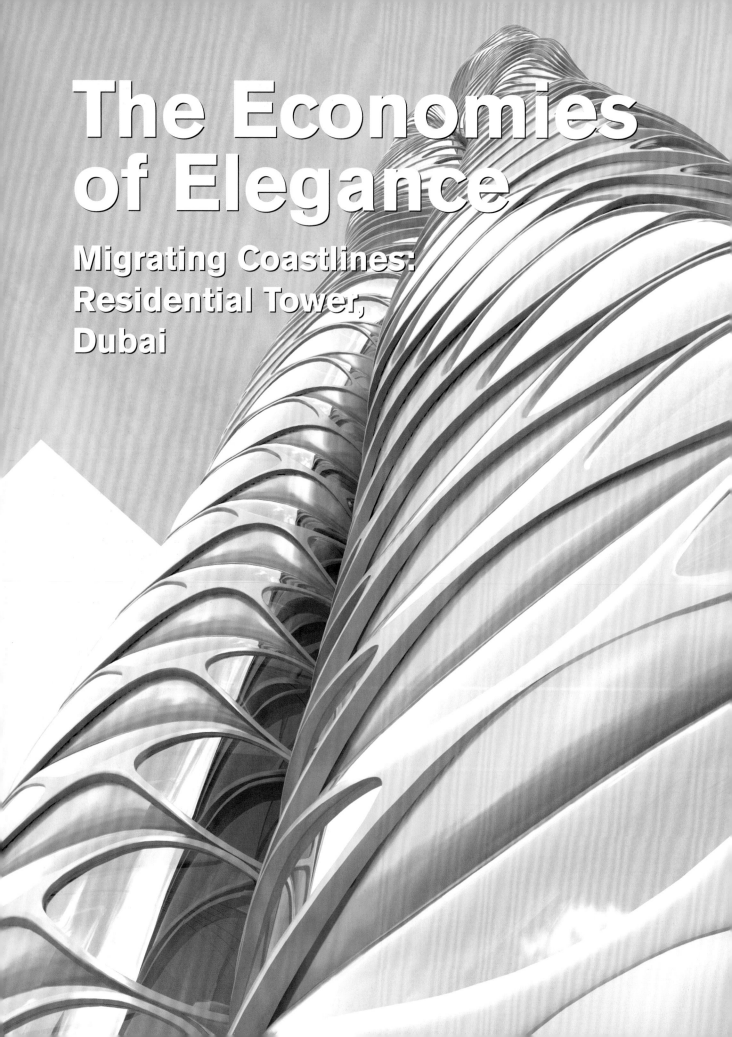

The Economies of Elegance

Migrating Coastlines: Residential Tower, Dubai

Ali Rahim and **Hina Jamelle** of Contemporary Architecture Practice describe how they have been able to design distinct features into their residential tower in Dubai that imbue its complex architecture with a rich aesthetic sensibility. Their skilful use of the digital algorithm has enabled them not only to develop interrelated models that allow for the collaboration of different industries, but also to deliver elegance to a construction budget. It is a design strategy that has further assisted in the development and implementation of innovative marketing techniques for the sale of individual apartments.

This 45-storey, 41,800-square-metre (450,000-square-foot) residential tower incorporates multiple levels of architectural complexity in its design, manufacturing and assembly. The design of the structure is based on a transformation of four tubes – three interior and one exterior – which integrates all of the mechanical and electrical systems. As it transforms, it opens to allow light to penetrate to the interior. The integration continues in the development of techniques that enable the fabrication and assembly of all building systems. Through its capacity to be adjusted and fine-tuned interactively, the design creates varied unit types that provide opportunities for new real-estate sales models based on qualities and potentialities of spaces rather than simply square footage. Economy at the scales of assembly and manufacturing, combined with the provision for innovative approaches to unit sales, allow for the development of elegance in a cost-effective way.

The building overlooks the city of Dubai and the Persian Gulf on one side and the desert on the other. Located on

Ali Rahim and Hina Jamelle/Contemporary Architecture Practice, Migrating Coastlines: Residential Tower, Dubai, United Arab Emirates, 2005–
The tower overlooks the city of Dubai and the Persian Gulf on one side and the desert on the other. The project attempts to engage in Dubai's status as a regional economic hub and as a haven for foreign nationals seeking to invest abroad and to escape political unrest at home.

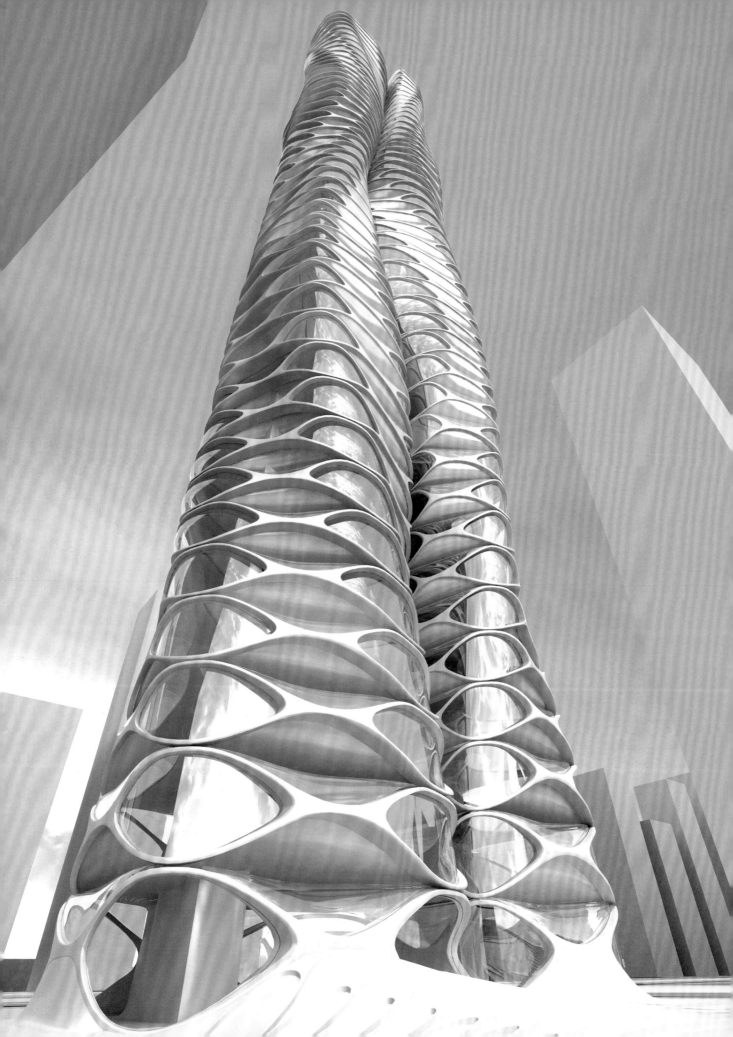

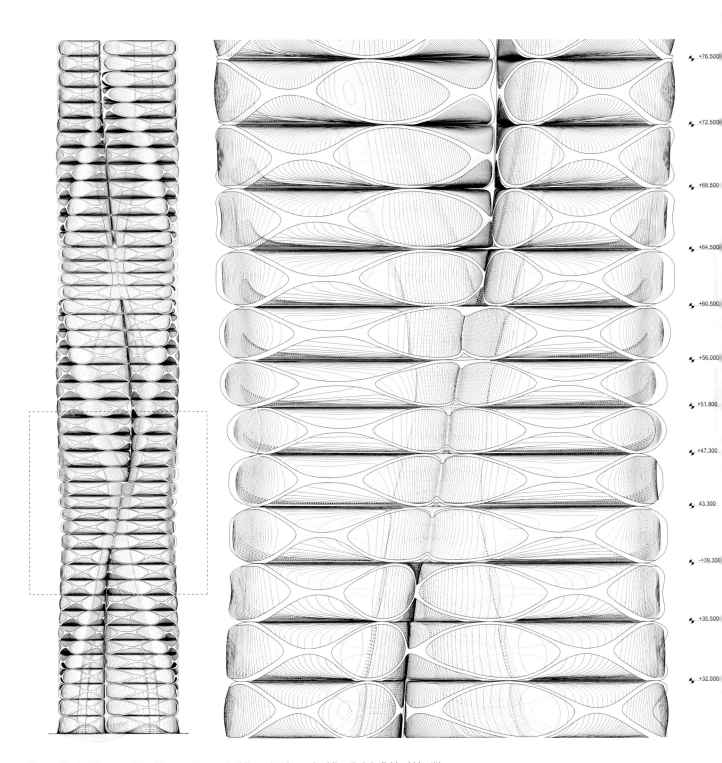

+76.500

+72.500

+68.500

+64.500

+60.500

+56.000

+51.800

+47.300

43.300

+39.300

+35.500

+32.000

Above: The building consists of two contiguous buildings that fuse, shedding their individual identities.
Opposite: By increasing exchanges with both its residents and the larger city, the building aims to facilitate a series of migrations whether human, economic or architectural. Several features at the base of the tower may serve to draw commerce away from the main street towards the desert, possibly increasing the value of land behind the building.

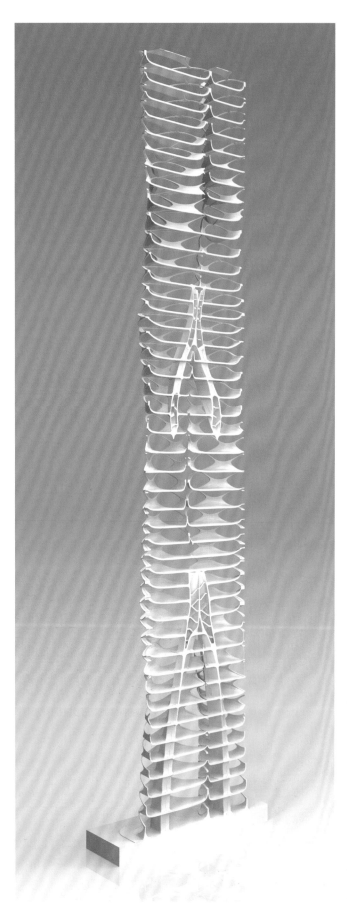

Sheikh Zayed Road – the main thoroughfare connecting Dubai and Abu Dhabi – the project attempts to engage Dubai's status as a regional economic hub and as a haven for foreign nationals seeking to invest abroad and to hedge political unrest at home. By catalysing exchanges with both its residents and the larger city, it aims to facilitate a series of migrations, whether human, economic or architectural.

To incorporate the myriad economic factors and site relationships into the design, the goal was to activate the middle section of the building, which from a real-estate perspective is typically considered least desirable. Each floor of the structure needed to respond to three desirable conditions: privacy between units, maximisation of views to the surrounding landscape, and the provision of several emergency exit paths. Twisting generated the tower's undulating profile – a vertical coastline marking the flows and migrations within the system that generated it. In addition, the middle floors of the building were compressed or shorter in height. As these new organisational patterns were guided by the decision-making process, new possibilities for the economic development of the middle section of the tower were developed.

The tower consists of two contiguous 45-storey buildings that fuse, shedding their individual identities. Each storey is developed into a variable module of concrete, glass and portions of a concrete structural core, an elevator shaft and emergency exit stairs. In aggregate, the variations between the modules produce the dynamic shape of the overall tower. The exterior glass walls are inflected, some curving outwards, the others remaining flat. The windows are clad in heat-sensitive low-iron glass that exhibits differing qualities depending on the location of the sun and amount of heat on its surface. The structural modules also twist over the height of the building, altering the load-bearing capacities of each floor. The elevator core stays roughly in the same position between floors, but the emergency stairs are torqued to maximise their potential utility.

The inflections in the building's envelope and cores cause the interior spaces to compress and expand from floor to floor, and the plan of each level is unique. On floors where the emergency stairs and elevator core are close together, the space in between may be used for storage; on the floors above, as the two cores move further apart, the interstitial area becomes larger and may create space for dining. The compression of the middle levels leads to units that have lower ceiling heights and are generally smaller and more affordable, alleviating the potential undesirability of the apartments on these floors.

The units in the tower thus avoid the repetition and sameness typical of high-rise residential buildings. Apartments range from studios to four-bedrooms and vary in size from 93 square metres (1,000 square feet) to 465 square metres (5,000

The transformation of an accumulative strategy of variations changes in kind when it transforms into the floor surface as well as into the structural tubes containing the stairs and elevator cores.

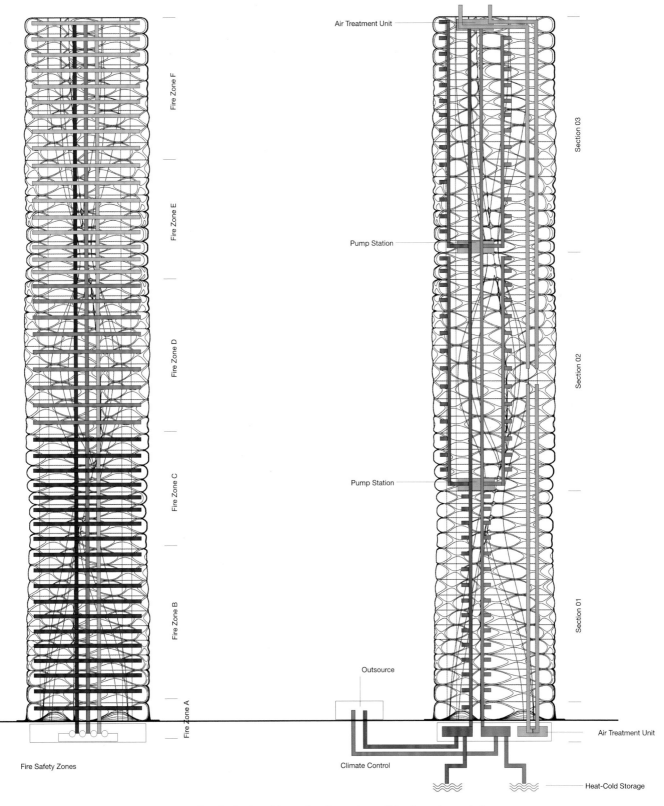

Fire Safety Zones

Fire Zone F

Fire Zone E

Fire Zone D

Fire Zone C

Fire Zone B

Fire Zone A

Air Treatment Unit

Pump Station

Pump Station

Outsource

Climate Control

Section 03

Section 02

Section 01

Air Treatment Unit

Heat-Cold Storage

Fire safety and mechanical systems integration. The distribution of the engineering systems will locate a primary plant on each of the technical floors. In this way the central plant is broken down to enable it to be sized for improved part-load performance and thereby increase its overall annual efficiency.

The glazing panels variation and fabrication is developed in one integrated interrelational model that transforms and adjusts, making modulations at all scales from floor-to-floor heights to the glass curvatures, and relating it directly to an updated building cost. This is done by collaborating directly with the concrete fabricators and glass manufacturers, yielding a cost for each trade as well as for the entire project.

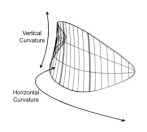

Glazing Panel Curvatures

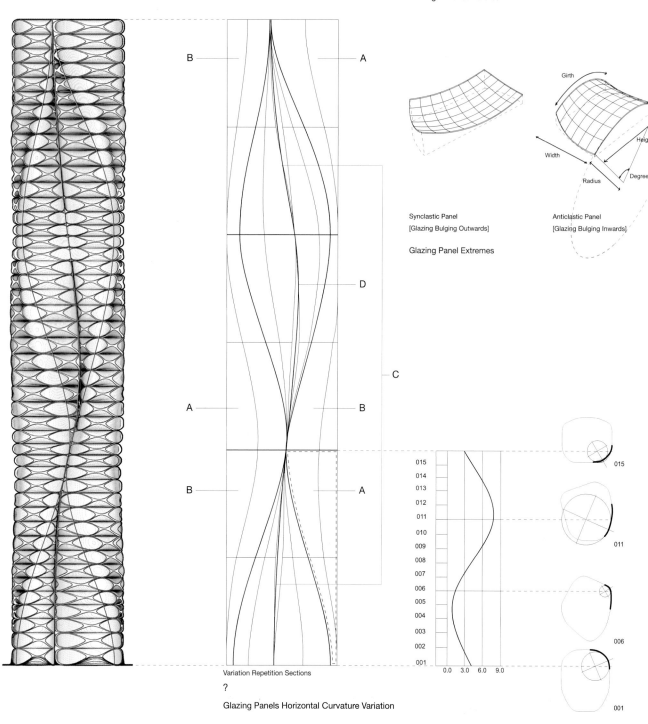

Synclastic Panel
[Glazing Bulging Outwards]

Anticlastic Panel
[Glazing Bulging Inwards]

Glazing Panel Extremes

Variation Repetition Sections

?

Glazing Panels Horizontal Curvature Variation

square feet). However, the complex inflections of spaces, room sizes, ceiling heights and apartment organisations makes it impossible to standardise marketing descriptions (for example, 'two-bedroom'). Instead, each apartment affords[1] a range of conditions and possibilities for occupation that expands the developer's options for marketing the units.

The relationships between structure, emergency stair core and unit change not only between floors, but also in response to the unique effects of each user. For example, the curvature of the exterior glass windows generates effects that change in relation to the perspective of inhabitants and passers-by moving within or past the building. As the building's envelope and spaces shift, twist and rotate, they produce migrating effects in perception and use. At a larger scale these perceptual and occupational effects may attract other foreign nationals to purchase units in the building. Hence the formation has the potential to inflect local migration patterns and to be transformed by changing occupancies.

The migration is also developed into interrelational models of the fabrication of the systems that are done off site. The model developed with the collaboration of glass manufacturers and concrete fabricators in Guangdong, China, is responsive and specific to the cost of glass and its curvature. The glass is linked to the overall building form, and as the form is changed so is the glass. In addition to this change in the direct relationship, the relationship of all of the other glass pieces also changes. This zone of influence of a particular change is designed to be gradual to maintain the aesthetic elegance of the project while also modulating the tower and the curvature of glass to make it affordable.

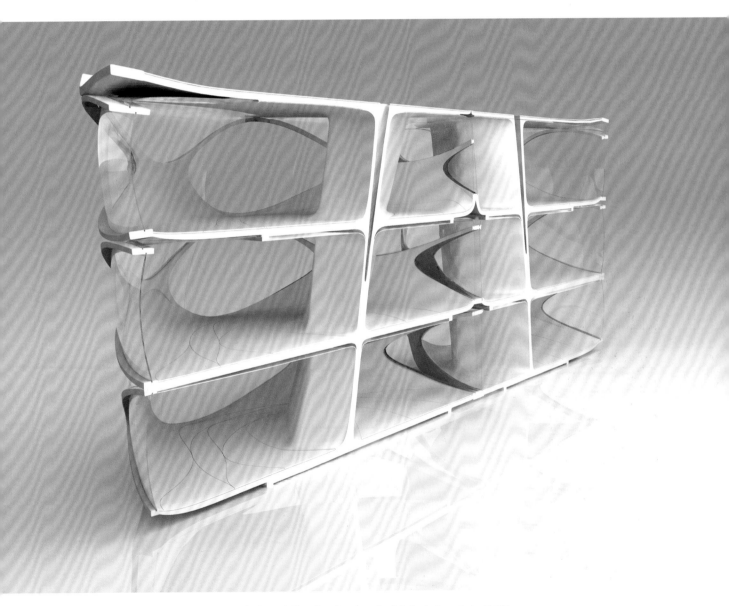

A close-up view of the section of the project reveals the mutation of surface from the interior to the exterior shells which are porous to allow light to penetrate the structural skin.

The building also contains effects in relation to its site. Several features at the base of the tower may serve to draw commerce away from Sheikh Zayed Road and towards the desert, possibly increasing the value of the land behind the tower and producing another migrating coastline. Amenities at the base include ponds that create a cool environment and power outlets that may facilitate the gathering of markets. The exact outcomes generated by such affordances depend on the specific behaviours of users. The intention, however, is to provide the potential of shifting economic exchanges and openness towards the desert.

By suggesting a new approach to selling real estate – in terms of quality and the potentials of space rather than just square footage – the design of the tower may influence how developers build and market condominiums in the future. The formation includes a series of migrating coastlines that reflect and shape the resettlement patterns of its residents – specifically, their attempts to gain residency in the UAE by purchasing real estate in Dubai. And the tower inflects the local economic conditions of Sheikh Zayed Road, potentially shifting the relationship between the desert and the city. △⊃

Note
1. Ali Rahim, *Catalytic Formations, Architecture and Digital Design*, Routledge (New York), 2006, pp 138–9

Above: Exterior view showing a gradient of transformation that migrates in the form of the tower as well as across the facade of the tower, producing elegant sensations.
Opposite: Interior view of the integration of lighting and floor pattern in a transforming surface.

Performing Elegance

At the level of global culture, the impact of elegant buildings is magnified where there is a seamless integration of complex parts and fabrication expressed through a mastery of techniques and transformative set of features. **Hani Rashid** of Asymptote explains how, in working at an international scale, the practice is now seeking to propagate innovative design through a 'developed understanding of the multiple levels of local responses that affect both local and global conditions'.

Notions of elegance in architecture have traditionally differed across cultural lines and distinctions, specific eras and nuances of locality and place. Today the advent of societies predicated on a new condition of hypermobility has caused a blurring of traditional boundaries and formed hybridised cultures with new concepts of what constitutes elegance in design, architecture and urbanism. With the propagation of the international style, the question of elegance in architecture and urbanism has been very precisely delineated within the bounds of mid-20th-century 'internationalism'. The recent onslaught of globalisation has subsequently produced a new and comparatively distorted space of elegance somewhere between the expected and the banal, the new and the unanticipated. It is within this emerging and convoluted context that one might begin to configure a new and even problematic definition of elegance.

As information streams speed past us, the electrosphere inundates us and delirium feeds our predisposition to spatiality and form a new understanding of elegance is emerging. It is within these residual territories of late modernity that one may begin to conceive new and divergent models for elegance. Elegance constituted of mathematical determinants, figurative ambiguity and informational effects are but a few of these new-found orders. Such new notions of elegance exploit today's conditions of fluidity and flux, seamlessness and the resulting abstractions of form and figure that are surfacing from many places within architectural theory and production. This space that engulfs and enfolds us today is saturated in prospects for such elegance, where expressions of cultural exchange and the aberrations caused by new assemblies of cultural production fold upon each other affording inspiration for new notions of what constitutes elegance.

The cities we occupy now both virtually and in reality are the very places in which this potential elegance is manifesting itself in various forms, from the mediated to the tectonic. And within this contemporary condition, architecture can aspire to new qualities that reside within conditions of indeterminacy, complexity and mutation. It is within parameters such as these that the intricacies of today's global culture forge a new sort of elegance, a space where innovation and progress in architectural terms propagate an elegance that is revealed from within the folds of the new. Within the global context, it is the contemporary architectural works that seek out innovation. Such notions of a new elegance are therefore distinguishable and far more important than the works adhering to the lingering reactionary forces in many modern cities where

Asymptote, Carlos Miele Flagship Store, New York, US, 2003
Previous spread: The design and architecture of the store embraces a culture that champions elegant aesthetics while being steeped in traditional cultural rituals and aesthetics, aspects that are also found in Miele's (a designer of Brazilian descent) own work.
Right: The interior is a hybrid of both a shopping environment and a sophisticated and sculpted backdrop against which to display.

The architecture is a 'place' for the rituals of gathering, meandering and viewing set against a landscape that celebrates desire and the sensual.

The overall atmosphere of the space is shaped as much by the exuberant vivacity of Brazilian culture as it is by the coolness and precision afforded by new technological means of fabrication, reflected in both the clothes and architectural elements.

This contemporary setting of seemingly disparate but not irreconcilable opposites influences and sets the stage for the presentation of Miele's *oeuvre*, creating a compelling spatial and visual experience.

misplaced obsessions with locality and identity promote an anachronistic idea of elegance as determined by 'good taste'.

This conservative and persistent idea of the perceived failure of 20th-century 'internationalism' to engage the nuances of locality and difference has spawned an architecture and urbanism that is symptomatically uninspired and rife with banality, a resulting condition that is perhaps ironically best described as 'inelegant'. However, such reactionary positions, which would deprive 21st-century cities of a necessary vitality, are now being challenged by the seemingly contentious and defiant reactionary attitudes and dictates of taste.

Elegance cannot therefore be thought of as a mere aesthetic or stylistic condition. Rather, a new elegance is emerging from more profound aspects tied to technological innovation coupled with a questioning of the status quo and a greater understanding of the multiple levels of contextual response. While cities such as Zurich, Paris and London seem to be trapped in the inertia of their bourgeois resistance to such new elegance, a breed of 'new' cities that one could say are situated at the leading edge of the present, cities such as Shanghai, Dubai and Singapore, are embracing technological innovation and experimentation as they are propelled towards some new form of the future. As many European centres struggle to maintain the facade and delusion of an elegant past, the conventional thinking and historically laden bias of their proponents are quick to denounce these 'new'

cityscapes. And yet it is precisely within this perceived 'inelegance', the rampant unbridled growth of cities such as Dubai or of the hyper-skylines of cities like Shanghai, that the potential may reside.

Certain forms of urban and technological experimentation and their subsequent applications, particularly in such contexts, will inevitably offer up new-found possibilities to perform architectures that embrace such a new elegance. Obviously these outcomes will subscribe to very different definitions and notions of what actually constitutes elegance. Here, taste, classical notions of beauty, proportions, historic references, pastiche, aesthetic frivolity and the like will inevitably be usurped by the tenants of a new elegance, where elegant solutions, elegant technologies and uses of such technologies in buildings, elegant environmental solutions, elegant structural engineering and new forms and aesthetics are influenced and propagated through mathematics and the use of nonstandard techniques. A new elegance in architecture is ultimately a manifestation of melding cultural significance with the inspired beauty locked within the natural technological and mathematical parameters that have always been architecture's underpinning and scaffold. ⌀

Text © 2007 John Wiley & Sons Ltd. Images © Asymptote: Hani Rashid and Lise Anne Couture, photos Paul Warchol, courtesy of Carlos Miele

Deus Ex Machina

From Semiology to the Elegance of Aesthetics

Architecture's ability to realise large-scale effects permits its emphasis to shift aesthetics on a project-by-project basis. Elegance unleashes a specific visual intelligence that can be achieved by refinement and precision of surface. Here, Mark Foster Gage investigates how elegance can be designed into a project. This requires a 'visual and formal expertise' combined with a careful curation of mutation and awareness of 'extreme differentiation'. Elegance often only reveals itself partially, acquired, in the design stage, through 'isolated views and expertly calibrated moments' and perceived fleetingly in built work.

Architecture has had its share of aesthetic design theories in the past – so why elegance, and why now? Modernism and its successors even seem at odds with the elegant as, for most of the 20th century, they rarely dabbled in the loquaciousness of adjectives. Instead, under the guise of supposed conflicts, architecture has lovingly endured decades of both Postmodernism's and critical Modernism's myopic interest in signification and semiotic content, whether indexical, iconic or symbolic.[1]

Choked with this need for signification, and bound by demands of economic and performance-based efficiencies, architecture has been excluded from the discourses of the aesthetic for nearly a century. It seems unlikely that digital technologies would be responsible for a 21st-century rebirth of aesthetics as a discourse, and even less likely that one of the first aesthetic judgements to emerge from this hiatus would be the historically aureate elegance – if for no other reason than its previously, and even distasteful, historical associations with the elite.

However, for the project of architectural formalism, a new aesthetic elegance is a clear and understandable direction. The supple surfaces, flowing vectors and allusions to movement enabled through topological and animate modelling technique point clearly to a novel sensuousness of form, an eroticism of plasticity awaiting some future critical encounter. But surely i cannot be enough to desire only the smooth[2] sensuousness of continuously undifferentiated surfaces – and even structures that are 'continuously connected and intertwined through fine-grain local linkages'[3] that emerged from the pivotal discourse of 'Animate Form'[4] and were elaborated in that of 'Intricacy'[5] seem to crave a more encompassing narrative of aesthetics for their continuing enrichment.

Architecture now needs qualifiers, such as elegance, less as descriptors and more as aspirations enlisted for the production of new effects.[6] An increasingly architecturally savvy public has been misled by the guise of a false contemporaneity in what Charles Jencks plainly terms 'Iconic Buildings'.[7] Like gremlins, art museums, libraries and concert

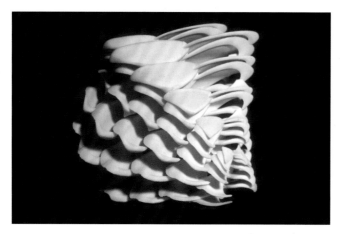 

Renee Lee, Ali Rahim Studio, University of Pennsylvania, Philadelphia, US, 2006
Left: A three-dimensional transformation yields differentiation in space and in surface articulation of the exterior envelope, achieving a mutation as one rotates around the building – a sophisticated and nuanced transformation.
Right: Close-up view of the surface migrating at a slow rate of change into a change in type beyond.

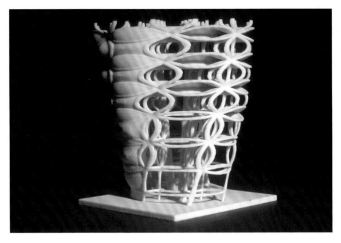

Shiying Liu, Ali Rahim Studio, University of Pennsylvania, 2006
Left: A generated accumulative model using scripting which is mediated by the subdivision of surfaces.
Right: A set of transformations that yields new surfaces.

halls, with their star-studded pedigrees, continue to propagate in every metropolis as a fictional relief from generations of aesthetically and effectually inert development. As an antidote to satisfying such a hunger with mere optical[8] novelty, or as Peter Eisenman observes the 'saccharine confections'[9] that these icons tend to become, there must be a larger visual discourse under which this new work is subsumed.

This initial premise, put forth by elegance and, by extension, a contemporary aesthetics, is that there is another objective emerging, like a literary *deus ex machina*,[10] from the retirement of the semiological – one larger and more encompassing than what would otherwise be dismissed as a mere formalist paroxysm. This new intent dismisses the need for semiological content, and replaces it with a new species of visual intelligence, sophisticated and nuanced, and designed towards the production of new aesthetically enabled effects,[11] such as elegance, aimed not at semiological satisfaction, but instead obsessed with the intricacies of aesthetic legibility and its affiliated production of desire.

The effect of elegance, with this ambition in mind, is not merely a contemporary substantive aesthetic judgement.[12] It is also a didactic and digestible architectural recipe. The production of elegance in this scenario requires not only techniques, but a visual and formal expertise. A truly expert and contemporary elegance cannot be generated from simple allusions to movement, sensuousness or fluidity, but also requires the production of desirable, yet sometimes mutant, anomalies that are curated to further exaggerate these, and other, aesthetic effects. Continuously variable forms provide degrees of sameness and difference, though rarely, without expert intervention, produce new emergent figural mutations within the system. This ability to curate mutation, and the production of emergent figures at multiple scales, is fundamental to contemporary elegance.

Elegance requires differentiation, but flourishes on mutation. Mutation, at its base level, is an evolution

technique for the production of potentially useful anomalies. It exists when an offspring has a genetic trait produced by a new DNA sequencing that does not exist in the parent.[13] Unfortunately, 'mutation' is also one of the most debased terms within the glossary of contemporary architecture, being mistakenly used as a synonym for individuation. A clarification of the term reveals that mutation enables future differences between species, while individuation identifies individuals within a subspecies or group. Different markings on the wings of butterflies provide a means for individuation, a mutation of those wings, which unlike a mere individuation can lead to the production of an entirely new species of butterfly. Differentiated components, coupled with isolated and extreme mutations resulting in new figures, produce the aesthetic effect of elegance.

Architectural mutation, in the absence of true evolutionary influences and detached from its misuse as individuation and differentiation, requires an anticipatory intervention on the part of the designer to produce a desirable anomaly distinct enough to be legible as a mutation and not merely read as individuation. In this light, animation software easily enables changes in degree within successive components, or individuation, within a family. Elegance requires extreme differentiation or, rather, a change in degree that verges on, or commits to, a change in type – a mutation. Continuously differentiated components are legible as variations of a primitive form, but do not produce the emergence of new figures and traits and cannot therefore produce architectural elegance. That is to say, their similarities overcome their differences. The assembly of different types of components results only in collage – or a circumvention of sameness through excessive difference. Contemporary elegance requires the expert calibration of these two extremes to produce figural mutations that become legible as sensuous effects. The perfection of the hermetically sealed topological system then allows these mutations to be registered as a new species of

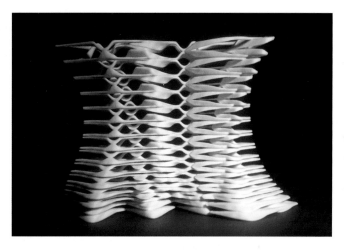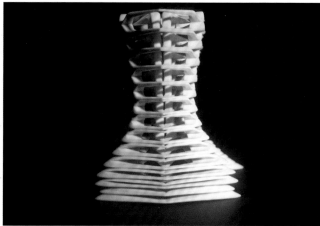

ChungYeon Won, Ali Rahim Studio, University of Pennsylvania, 2006
Left: A gradient transformation yielding larger spaces as it migrates vertically, allowing for the different inhabitation of a mixed-use programme to occur in different areas of the building.
Right: Detail view showing different scales of transformation within the building.

emergent figure, not component and not whole, but existing as an ephemeral fugitive in between the two extremes.

The consensus use of surface modelling software authorises the legibility of the mutation. Such design systems include an implicit mathematical framework that provides for a common standard of architectural production not available to architects since the early 20th-century extermination of the classical.[14] The renewed adoption of such a consensus-based approach to design is critical for the production of contemporary elegance as it alone provides the datum against which an expertly curated anomaly can be recognised. The establishment of such a datum, combined with an expert use of techniques, allows for not only the recognition of the parts as individual components, and their intricate assembly as wholes, but also enables a vast range of intermediary scale effects – vis-à-vis these mutations. These elegant effects exist between clear readings of parts and wholes, and between distinctions such as surface articulation and mass. Elegant design effects produce a new family of intermediary tropes that augment the limited aspirations of both efficient assemblies of standardised parts and talented compositions of complete wholes.

The interest of elegance, as one of a new generation of charismatic and contemporary[15] effects, relies on the presence of figuration. As such, a critical aspect of defining elegance is determining the type of figures that result in its realisation. Other emerging positions, such as the techno-romantic and the horrific, rely on the extreme production of figural geometries that disempower a formational legibility of wholeness. In both cases the means of viewership is cinematic, allowing for a sequential reading of figure through figure, and figure against figure. Elegance requires the topological framework against which a figure can be read. It is not cinematic in its ambitions, but rather curated through isolated views and expertly calibrated moments. Unveiled not through the movement of the body, but rather through the long caress

of a continuous visual appraisal, elegance is statuesque in its retrieval and delicate in its aesthetic presumptions.

Because of its reliance on the visual and aesthetic, as opposed to the conceptual and semiological, contemporary elegance is a localised occurrence. Only a retreat from reading a building as a complete conceptual entity allows for the emergence of elegant effects. A building may exhibit elegance at a variety of scales, but it is always, and only, accessible as a locally specific occurrence. It is therefore permanent, but not omnipresent, always available yet experientially fleeting. This is the sacrifice of all sensate-based interests – and like all good sacrifices it enables the possibility of an alternate, and better, opportunity. Its potency is generated not through its eternal conceptual legibility, but rather through a visceral precognitive and momentary realisation.[16] It is a 'flash in the pan',[17] a powerful observation made all the more persuasive precisely because of its brevity. Elegance is reproducible at any scale, in any topological scenario, but it cannot be everywhere, always. It is, in this sense, an ephemeral effect, but one that can be rehearsed. Architecture is uniquely poised to capitalise on this rehearsal as part of its disciplinary specificity which has historically relied on an implicit assumption of permanence and stasis – allowing elegance to be perceptually fleeting yet architecturally predictable through curating views with expert manipulations of form.

These emerging aesthetic desires of architecture provide a new and common denominator for the discourse not available to architects since the early 20th century. Also emerging from this aesthetic consensus, as well as the unified use of tools and techniques, is the reintroduction of nuance and an extreme degree of individual sophistication. After its disappearance for decades, we now realise that formal nuance is impossible without group expertise that allows for its recognition. These emerging aesthetic tendencies and consensus use of tools demand a new aesthetic discourse.

Elegance, as the ability to expertly integrate dissonant mutations towards the production of effect, expands the previously limited aesthetic range of digital formalism. In this capacity it is an important initial direction within the nascent discourse of aesthetics and architectural affects.

It is *en vogue* now for architects to study infrastructure, globalisation, marketing, branding and systems of commerce. It seems only fitting that a continuation of this research would inevitably lead back to the study of the architectural agency of desire, of which a significant portion must be aesthetic, as the driving force behind a significant percentage of this commercial and corporate activity. The study of aesthetics, including elegance effects, is not a careless disregard for conceptual semiological thinking, but rather heralds the production of a new and entirely contemporary species of intelligence – one not beholden to historical models of signification, but liberated and enabled by the ability to produce, control and understand a crucial aspect of the judgement and consumption of an architecture of irrefutable contemporaneity. ∆

Notes
1. Peter Eisenman writes: 'In the early 20th century, American pragmatist philosopher Charles Sanders Peirce put forward an articulate, three-part typology of signs: the icon, the symbol, and the index. The icon is distinguished by a similitude; it looks like its object, i.e., the hot dog stand that looks like a hot dog. The symbol is understood by convention or rule, like words in a sentence, or a classical façade symbolizing a public building … The last of Peirce's categories, the index, is understood as a record of a process or event.' Peter Eisenman, 'Duck Soup', in Cynthia Davidson (ed), *Log 7*, 2006, p 140.
2. Smoothness suggests a physical lack of articulation, but has also been enlisted architecturally as a theoretical distinction opposed to, but always in the presence of, the striated – architectural translations of the sedentary and nomadic. See Gilles Deleuze and Felix Guattari, *A Thousand Plateaus: Capitalism and Schizophrenia*, Athlone Press (London), 1988, p 478.
3. Greg Lynn, 'Intricacy', in *Intricacy: a Project by Greg Lynn FORM*, Institute of Contemporary Art (Philadelphia, PA), 2003, p 8.
4. See Greg Lynn, *Animate Form*, Princeton Architectural Press (New York), 1999.
5. See Greg Lynn, 'Intricacy', op cit, pp 8–10.
6. Jeffrey Kipnis notes that: 'To distinguish post-critical from pre-critical sensibilities and to call attention to the fact that the emotional impact of the work emanates not from the representations of the architecture but from the formal structures themselves, Eisenman termed these new sensations collectively as "affects"'. Jeffrey Kipnis, 'P-TR's Progress', in Todd Gannon (ed), *The Light Construction Reader*, Monacelli Press (New York), 2002, p 151.
7. See Charles Jencks, *The Iconic Building*, Rizzoli (New York), 2005.
8. Eisenman, op cit, p 140.
9. A reference by Peter Eisenman to the merely optical qualities of Santiago Calatrava's work. Ibid, p 41
10. A '*deus ex machina*' is a literary device whereby an unexpected, artificial or improbable character, device or event is suddenly introduced to resolve a situation or untangle a plot – as in the final battle sequence of *Monty Python and the Holy Grail* which is suddenly halted by the appearance of the modern-day police who arrest the entire cast of medieval characters for murder. See William Morris, *The American Heritage Dictionary*, 2nd college edn, Houghton Mifflin (Boston, MA), 1982.
11. Sylvia Lavin has provided perhaps the finest description of effects and their role in contemporary discourse. See Sylvia Lavin, 'In a contemporary mood', in Zaha Hadid and Patrik Schumacher (eds), *Latent Utopias: Experiments Within Contemporary Architecture*, Steirischer Harbst (Graz), 2002, p 46.
12. For a description of the differences between substantive and verdictive judgements, see Nick Zangwill, *The Metaphysics of Beauty*, 1st edn, Cornell University Press (Ithaca, NY), 2001, pp 9–10.
13. Morris, op cit.
14. For an articulate record of the threats to which classicism ultimately succumbed in the early 20th century, see the 'fallacies' in Geoffrey Scott, *The Architecture of Humanism: A Study in the History of Taste*, WW Norton (New York), 1999.
15. Lavin, op cit, pp 46–7.
16. Kant, in the first two moments of his 'Critique of Judgment', presents the requisite for this as 'subsuming under concepts', the critical switch that, at its base level, requires aesthetic judgement to occur independently of the act of cognition by the subject. Immanuel Kant, *The Critique of Judgment*, trans James Creed Meredith, 1st edn, Clarendon Press (Oxford), 1952, pp 41–60.
17. Sylvia Lavin aptly defines the fleeting aspects of the contemporary through the analogy of the 'flash in the pan'. Sylvia Lavin, 'Introduction', in Sylvia Lavin and Helene Furjan (eds), *Crib Sheets*, Monacelli Press (New York), 2005, pp 9–10.

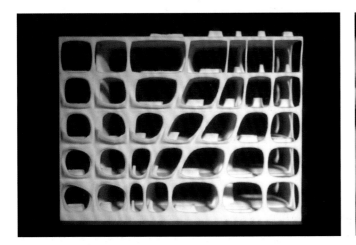
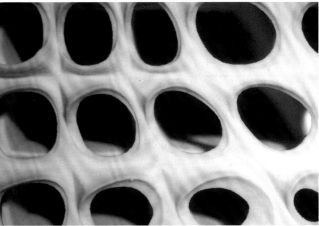

Paul Privitera, Ali Rahim Studio, University of Pennsylvania, 2006
Left: The mutation occurs as the external envelope meets the surface of the inhabitable surface, which is continually transformed as well.
Right: Detail view showing the delicate growth of the surface to create balconies or shading devices.

(K)not
a Loop

For **Meejin Yoon** of MY Studio the creation of a Möbius-strip dress was an opportunity to explore 'surface as a seamless transformative condition between interior and exterior'. It is a piece that through its differentiation and continuity of surface provides a wholly architectural interpretation of the elegant.

In examining the body and its material envelopes – skin, clothing and architecture – the relationship between surface and space comes into question as a conceptual and corporeal construct. The Möbius Dress uses the mathematical principle of the Möbius strip, a two-dimensional compact manifold with a single boundary component, to re-examine surface as a seamless transformative condition between interior and exterior. The project uses the topological principles of this one-sided, one-edged, non-orientable surface (a loop with a half-twist) as both envelope and spatial device.

Exploring and exploiting the continuity of this twisted, single-sided surface, the dress uses the generative logic of splitting to knot a series of occupiable spatial loops. Structured by the body, it is nondirectional in terms of form and materiality. By varying the parametric relationships between the measures of the body, splitting edge and surface area, the internal and external logics are intertwined to exact elegance. Splitting the Möbius strip reveals the simple rules and complex interrelationships between surface and space.

While the skin is the body's most immediate envelope, largest organ and most sophisticated container, clothing remains a constructed second skin limited to two-dimensional fabrication. Unlike the skin's continuous compound curvature of the body, clothing is made from flat, two-dimensional surfaces that are sewn, cut, pleated and darted to produce a three-dimensional form. The dress pattern itself is both a template and a manual – a complete construction document in which the surface is coded with a series of operational notations that enable the maker to move from the flatness of a two-dimensional surface into a three-dimensional form. The Möbius Dress is always already both a single surface and a three-dimensional form.

Redefining the relationship between inside and outside, and between internal organisation and external constraints, the Möbius Dress exemplifies a smooth, continuous, homogeneous surface that is simultaneously simple and complex. It exploits the surface logic of a one-sided, one-edged, non-orientable surface, clothing the body in a variable and evolving form, and applies the transformative potential of a half-twisted loop by exacting simple rules of splitting that allow the topological principles to not only become visible, but occupiable as the surface is split into knots.

Cutting a Möbius strip in half by cutting it along the middle, parallel to the edge, creates a strip twice as long with four half-twists. Cutting this new loop down the middle creates two strips linked around each other, each with four half-twists. Cutting the Möbius strip in thirds creates two linked loops, one with one half-twist, and one with four half-twists. This 'splitting rule' demonstrates that a strip with an even number, n, of half-twists creates two loops, each with n half-twists. If n is odd, it creates one loop with $2n + 2$ half-twists. Thus splitting becomes a generative procedure.

Exploiting these compound geometrical properties, the Möbius Dress exacts a continuously evolving surface in relationship to the body. It does not simply clothe the body by loosely paralleling contours, rather, it reveals its internal organisation through gradually transforming in relationship to the body. Its geometry follows a logic that is self-perpetuating, self-structuring yet externally constrained and adaptable to the body. The Möbius Dress splits, turns inside-out and forms two intertwined loops that conform to the body at different scales, meeting around the hips and torso, and is made of industrial recycled felt, a homogeneous and seamless material created through friction as opposed to weaving. The felt has no warp, no weft, no orientation and no hierarchy.

In order to clothe the body in a new type of garment – one that negotiates the internal logics of a two-dimensional compact manifold with the external constraints of a three-dimensional body – the Möbius Dress employs certain surface logics and material properties. The form of the dress as it unravels becomes differentiated, while the surface remains continuous. Applying a simple set of rules to an inherently supple geometry, the project challenges the conventional understanding of envelope as a delimiting condition. Using technique not only to rethink the stable separation of inside and outside, but to investigate new spatial possibilities, the principles of the Möbius Dress provoke a rethinking of architecture as stable limits, suggesting instead a more smooth and seamless understanding of interiority and exteriority. △

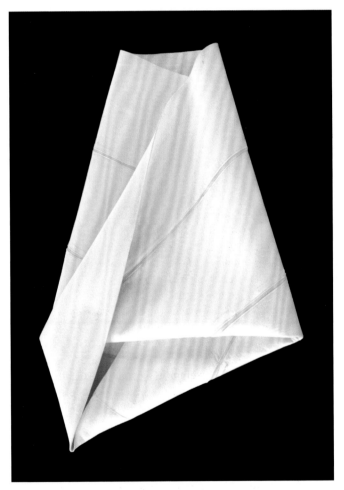

MY Studio, Möbius Dress, Boston, Massachusetts, US, 2005
Left: The dress without a body to structure reveals the half-twist and an inside-out fold.
Right: As the dress splits into two interlocked loops, the body structures and restructures the form of the garment.
Opposite: The Möbius Dress is made of recycled industrial felt, which is nondirectional. The material has no warp or weft and uses custom-length zippers along the 'splitting' edges to unravel into loops.

Notes on Designing Surficial Elegance

Mastery of technique is as essential as design ability to the production of elegant works. Elegant features can only be realised through an understanding of the systemic logics of the digital environment and a full working knowledge of generative techniques. Benjamin H Bratton of The Culture Industry and Hernan Diaz Alonso of Xefirotarch describe Xefirotarch's wholly visceral, but exacting, approach to the design process.

Mayan Cinema

Xefirotarch's design obsessions are based on an appreciation for the perversity of elegant form, a taste learned from the movies and set to work on architecture. This said, perhaps its architecture is itself elegant. Perhaps when the projected figure is frozen in a sufficiently dense, opulent articulation it does achieve a resonant state of elegance. But if so, such an achievement derives as much from the act of designing the figure as it does from the intensity of the extant form.

It is produced in the act of design, less through special techniques or processes than through the focused sensation of pointing and clicking. Here, the sensation is more like painting than engineering – driven by personal, idiosyncratic gesture more than an application of systematic procedure to material condition.

The genesis of this is internally driven, but not intuitive. Having watched hours, weeks, months of Bad Hitchcockian cinema, Hernan Diaz Alonso's microtechniques for combing the thresholds of the horrific-becoming-elegant and the elegant-becoming-horrific have imprinted themselves as visual-temporal cues on his design retina. These codes (cut here, blend there, match-on-action, shot-reverse-shot, false POV, staccato violins, and so on) are processed, mashed up and reprojected back onto the screen space of animation software.

Here, image forms are densely layered and then pulled back from themselves, balanced and unbalanced, so that their formal 'architecture' within the frame always competes with the strictures of the edit – the latent seam – for the organisation of the screen event. In the course of such moments, Diaz Alonso is director, editor and audience all at once, watching the form materialise and interacting with this emergence. His decisions to speed up and slow down, slice and blend, fuse and separate, are repetitions of the scenic rhythms he has learned from a lifetime of being awed by cinematic effect.

This is visceral. Like the film-goer engrossed within the cinematic apparatus of yore (see Baudry, Deleuze and Penley), this well-immersed designer sweats and squirms and grunts over what he watches before him. This is an exacting processing behaviour, like the subconscious mind during the dream state, cycling through the raw data of everyday life, cutting and pasting, iterating towards multiple provisional renders on the mind's eye.

The designer settles into the liminal consciousness of productive concentration, into an unfolding practice that is also a kind of cinema played out on the cameras obscura of his glowing monitors. Any elegance that is read within the final render is an index of the precision of such processing. ∆

Xefirotarch, Art Hotel, Puerto Plata, Dominican Republic, 2005
The Art Hotel is a luxuriously unlikely form, a frothing precious metal emerging from the profit (excess) of the multiple economies of exclusivity, leisure and refined exclusion that would enable it, and be cited (sited) through it.

Fabricating Elegance
Digital Architecture's Coming of Age

For **Joseph Rosa**, John H Bryan Curator of Architecture at the Institute of Chicago, elegance with its 'refined aesthetic ability' represents a concurrent maturing of design culture and technologies. It builds on the pioneering fabrication techniques of the late 1990s, spearheaded in seminal projects such as the Korean Presbyterian Church in New York by Greg Lynn, Douglas Garofalo and Michael McInturf, and the Yokohama Port Terminal by Foreign Office Architects.

dECOi, Paris duplex, France, 2003
View from the living room to the dining area beyond with an elongated contiguous fireplace hearth that was digitally conceived and fabricated at a refinery.

The word 'elegance' has many connotations, but is most frequently used to describe a style and appearance that is refined and mature in character. While the use of the term has, for the most part, applied to fashion, where elegance is synonymous with *haute couture* and the couturier's art of making, it can also be associated with architecture.

Most recently, the term has been used to describe a select type of built architecture that originates from the realm of digital ideology and is reflected in realised projects by Zaha Hadid, UNStudio, Foreign Office Architects, Greg Lynn, Ross Lovegrove and Yves Behar. Here it describes a matured sense of production that informs and merges materiality with formal qualities. Elegance in digital architecture operates in a post-technique era that addresses issues of aesthetics and subjectivity while forging a new direction of thinking and production for the avant-garde.

As with any ideology or art movement, it proceeded along a trajectory of progressions to more established methods and techniques, and then to a more refined aesthetic sensibility. Sometimes in these lineages the avant-garde thinking that originally marked its arrival is subsumed and normalised into a perfected model that loses any sense of its original progressive ideology. Hence matured aesthetic sensibility that has no trace of its avant-garde origins. However, with digital ideology the avant-garde has always been integral to the rethinking and refining of its evolution in the pedagogy and practice of architecture.

Digitally informed practice has included many generations of designers since its arrival in the early 1990s, so it is not new to the discourse of architecture, and has a history. In reviewing the history of the work produced in this field, the level of technological development and the quality of the

A digitally augmented metal panel hangs from the ceiling, separating the bathroom from the dressing area.

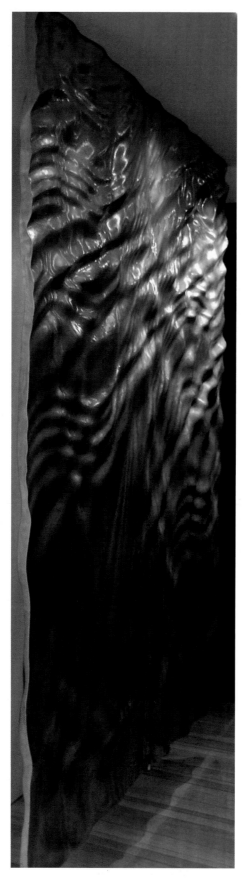

dECOi, Paris duplex.

constructed work cannot be separated. As techniques have been further refined and improved, so has the quality of the fabricated work and its aesthetic sensibility. In many ways, the fabrication of digital architecture is a metanarrative for fashion, where *haute couture* designers cannot operate without a high-quality couturier to fabricate the idea.

An example of this is the 1999 Korean Presbyterian Church in Queens, New York, designed collaboratively by Greg Lynn, Douglas Garofalo and Michael McInturf. The church is one of the earliest and largest examples of digital ideology in architecture. While some of the early digital modelling images of the project might, in retrospect, appear primitive in comparison with today's highly developed digital techniques, when it was designed and built this building was the most avant-garde example of digital literacy transitioning from its pedagogical roots into the realm of critical practice. At the time, however, the simple act of using digitally informed machinery to crimp or bend the edge of a building material was not especially feasible.

The next milestone was Foreign office Architects' 2002 Yokohama Port Terminal in Yokohama, Japan. The roof of this vast structure is a public park that allows this seasonally used pier to be active year round. To achieve its built folded form, FOA employed shipbuilding techniques, which produced a more refined crimped edging, to fabricate the building's massive sections, which were then assembled at the site. Both the Korean Presbyterian Church and the Yokohama Port Terminal buildings are sequential models of achievement in the history of digital ideology and its translation into built structures.

Numerous other projects have since been realised in this idiom. However, there are no definitive models that epitomise acts of fabrication, simply because the methodologies and fabrication techniques have become highly refined and a standard in the discourse. Therefore, in this post-technique stage, it is essential that the aesthetic intention informs the quality of its production and the ideology of the movement – hence, digital elegance. This is most evident in the blurred boundaries between the disciplines of architecture and industrial design, which can operate at the same scale for ideological explorations and result in fabricated buildings or objects.

One aspect of this can be found in Zaha Hadid's 2005 Phaeno Science Centre in Wolfsburg, Germany. The building's monocoque-like concrete massing is visually supported by tapered piers that are similar in character to the legs designed for her 2005 Aqua Table, manufactured by Established & Sons. Hadid's ideology operates at the same scale of intention. However, once transposed to a medium – a building or a table – materiality and fabrication inform its character. An early sign of this way of thinking is evident in her 2000 Z-Scape Furniture manufactured by Sawaya & Moroni. The sofa from this line is a sinuous, undulating, extruded form that embodies modern elegance. Clad in animal skin, its monochromatic colour allows the upholstered surfaces to accentuate the sofa's monolithic form.

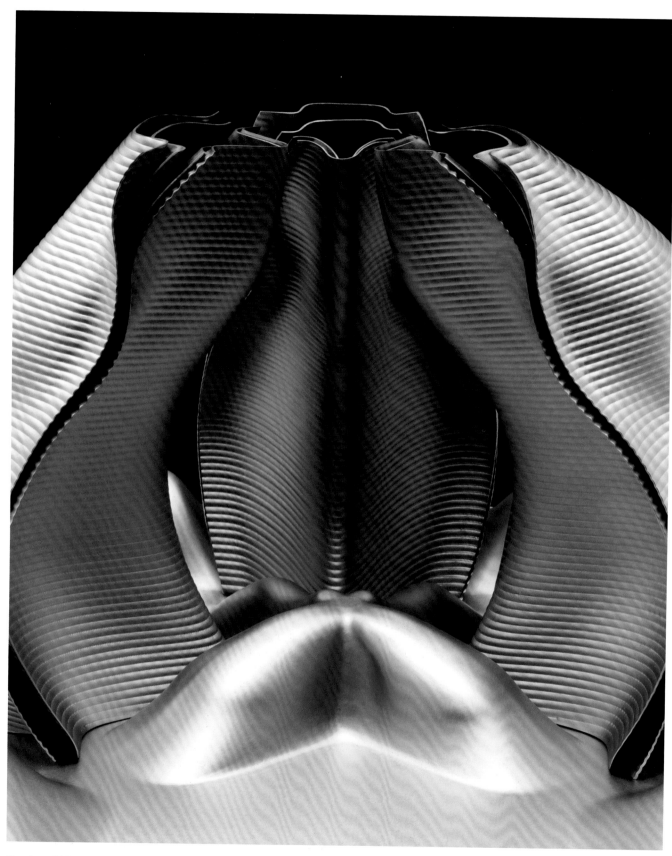

Greg Lynn FORM, 2003 Tea & Coffee Tower, manufactured by Alessi
Three of the five forms, which complete this monolithic shape, reveal their elegant profiles, which also produces a
hidden void space at the centre of the Tea & Coffee Tower.

Foreign Office Architects, Yokohama Port Terminal Building, Yokohama, Japan, 2002
View up from the perimeter exterior circulation ramp that descends into the central interior space of the building.

The formal aesthetics of built digital elegance are also seen in Asymptote's 2003 Carlos Miele boutique in New York. Here the monocoque-like interior of the store visually disengages the visitor from rectilinear spatial constraints and formally engulfs the clothing that hovers over the floor. In fact, the only element that gives this space scale is the clothing.

This fusion between form and function in different scales of production is also illustrated in the evolution of Greg Lynn's architectural and industrial design works. Lynn's bilaterally symmetrical configured 2003 Tea & Coffee Tower, manufactured by Alessi, evokes a sense of opulence through its materials and refined fabrication process. The formal character of the object is very much influenced by his earlier 1999 Embryological House, which explored the digital possibilities of mass customisation for a domestic architecture.

Elegance in the realm of industrial design can also be seen in the ideology of Ross Lovegrove. His extensive line of 'Istanbul' bathroom fixtures (2006), manufactured by Vitra, demonstrates a refined aesthetic sensibility that moves beyond the minimal modern aesthetic into a new realm of emotive forms that are both elegant and organic in origin. And in industrial designer Yves Behar's new 2006 Leaf Lamp for Herman Miller (2006), the lamp form physically transforms – depending on how one adjusts it – and merges the boundaries of aesthetics, innovative LED technology and digital fabrication into a single, cohesive, elegant form.

Many other designers are also reintroducing aesthetic subjectivity into their matured digital discourse, examples of which include dECOi's built duplex in Paris (2003), UNStudio's Mercedes-Benz Museum in Stuttgart (2006) and Contemporary Architecture Practice's Reebok flagship store in China (2007). Also encoding the characteristic of elegance in architectural production are Preston Scott Cohen's drawings for his Tel Aviv Museum of Art, and Lynn's exuberant interior fabrications for his Bloom House in Santa Monica, California, scheduled for completion in early 2007.

As digital architectural production matures into the historical canon along with its new-found alliance with industrial design ideology, the quality of aesthetics and fabrication is key to the further development of this avant-garde discourse. The same can historically be said of the fashion industry, where the quality of the couturier is essential for the aesthetics of *haute couture*'s existence as well as the fabrication of an elegance that is avant-garde. ∆

Contributors

Ben van Berkel and **Caroline Bos** set up their Architectuurbureau in Amsterdam in 1988. Among other projects, the firm has realised the Karbouw Office Building, the Erasmus Bridge in Rotterdam, Het Valkhof Museum in Nijmegen, the Möbius House and the NMR facilities for the University of Utrecht. In 1998 they established a new firm, UNStudio, which presents itself as a network of specialists in architecture, urban development and infrastructure. Current UNStudio projects include the restructuring of the station area of Arnhem, a new Mercedes-Benz Museum in Stuttgart, a music theatre for Graz, and the design and restructuring of the Harbor Ponte Parodi in Genoa. Van Berkel has lectured and taught at many architectural schools around the world, and is currently Professor of Conceptual Design at the Staedelschule in Frankfurt am Main. Central to his teaching is the inclusive approach of architectural works integrating virtual and material organisation and engineering constructions. Bos is an analyst involved in all UNStudio projects. She observes, studies and describes the different programmatic issues and communicates these directly with the different parties involved. She has taught as a guest lecturer at Princeton University, the Berlage Institute in Rotterdam, University of Applied Arts in Vienna and the Academy of Architecture in Arnhem.

Benjamin Bratton ia a theorist and strategist who uses architecture as a medium for nonarchitectural experiments. He is principal of The Cultural Industry, an interdisciplinary design and research consultancy based in Los Angeles, connecting investments in image, media and space. The firm's work links speculative programmatic narrrative systems and networked media, from software to cinema to architecture. Recent strategic planning clients have included Yahoo!, Microsoft, Motorola, Imaginary Forces and several global advertising agencies. Bratton was co-chair of 'Ambient:Interface', the 54th Annual International Design Conference in Aspen, Colorado. His publications range in topic from software theory to the mimetic logics of terrorism, including, most recently, 'The Logistics of Habitable Circulation', his introduction to Paul Virilio's *Speed and Politics* (Semitext(e)/MIT Press, 2006). He has taught at SCI-Arc and at UCLA since 2001.

Manuel DeLanda is the author of a number of books on philosophy including

War in the Age of Intelligent Machines (1992) and *A Thousand Years of Nonlinear History* (1997), both published by Zone Books, and *Intensive Science and Virtual Philosophy* (2002) and *A New Philosophy of Society* (2006), published by Continuum, as well as of many philosophical essays published in various journals and collections. He teaches two seminars at the University of Pennsylvania Department of Architecture: 'Philosophy of History: Theories of Self-Organization and Urban Dynamics', and 'Philosophy of Science: Thinking about Structures and Materials'.

Hernan Diaz Alonso is the principal and founder of Xefirotarch, an award-winning design firm in Los Angeles. He is also the thesis coodinator at SCI-Arc, and teaches studio design and visual studies at SCI-Arc and Columbia University. He has lectured widely around the world, and his work has been published in numerous books and major international publications. He recently received the YAP award for his warm-up pavilion at PS1 MoMA in New York (2005). His architectural designs have been shown at both architecture and art exhibitions, including the 2004 Venice Biennale of Architecture and the 2006 London Biennale. His first monograph is due to be published in early 2007.

Mark Foster Gage is the founding partner of Gage/Clemenceau Architects in New York, and an assistant professor of architecture at Yale University. His firm is a recognised pioneer in the field of integrating innovative computational and material technologies into the production of new, aesthetically performative directions for architecture. His projects, writings, exhibitions and research have been published in the *New York Times*, *LA Times*, *Vogue*, *Homme*, *Interior Design*, *Surface*, *A+U*, *Architecture*, *Metropolis*, *Architectural Record* and *JAE*. He is currently working on a book entitled *Performance Aesthetics*, funded by the A Whitney Griswold Faculty Research Fund.

David Goldblatt is a professor of philosophy at Denison University and is the author of *Art and Ventriloquism* (2005), part of Routledge's Critical Voices in Art, Theory and Culture Series. He also co-edited, with Lee B Brown, *Aesthetics: A Reader in Philosophy of the Arts* (Prentice Hall, 2005) and has published widely on the subjects of art and philosophy, especially architecture, in publications including *The Journal of Aesthetics and Art*

Criticism, *Philosophy and Film*, *The Southern Journal of Philosophy*, *Philosophy and Literature*, *The McNeese Review*, *Anfioni Zeto*, *Historical Reflections/Reflexions Historiques* and *Art Issues*. More recently he has contributed articles to Oxford University Press's *Encyclopedia of Aesthetics*, *The Encyclopedia of American Studies*, *What is Architecture?* (edited by Andrew Ballantyne) and *Bob Dylan and Philosophy*.

Zaha Hadid, Pritzker Laureate 2004, is an architect who consistently pushes the boundaries of architecture and urban design. Her central concerns involve a simultaneous engagement in practice, teaching and research. She is best known for her seminal built works: the Vitra Fire Station, Land Formation-One, Bergisel Ski-Jump, Strasbourg Tram Station, Rosenthal Centre for Contemporary Art in Cincinnati, BMW Central Building in Leipzig, Hotel Puerta America (interior) in Madrid, Ordrupgaard Museum Extension in Copenhagen, Phaeno Science Centre in Wolfsburg, and the Maggies Cancer Care Centre in Scotland. Her revolutionary design for the MAAXI Contemporary Arts Centre in Rome is scheduled for completion this year. She is currently a professor at the University of Applied Arts in Vienna, and was the Eero Saarinen Visiting Professor of Architectural Design at Yale.

Hina Jamelle is an architect and co-director of Contemporary Architecture Practice in New York (www.c-a-p.net). Prior to joining the practice in 2002 she was a client partner at Razorfish, a digital media consulting company. She teaches graduate architecture studios at the Pratt Institute and the University of Pennsylvania, and previously taught at the University of Michigan. Contemporary Architecture Practice's projects include a wide range and scales of work from product design to high-rises. Its work was most recently exhibited at the Museum of Modern Art (MoMA), New York, and the Entry 2006 Expo in Essen, Germany. Past exhibition venues include Artists Space, New York, the Royal Institute of British Architects (RIBA) and the London and Shanghai Architectural Biennales in 2005 and 2006.

Greg Lynn is the principal of Greg Lynn FORM and has taught throughout the US and Europe. He has taught and lectured around the world as the Professor of Spatial Conception and Exploration at the ETH in Zurich, and as an adjunct assistant professor at Columbia University. In the autumn of 2002 he became an o.univ. professor at the Angewandte in Vienna. In addition, he is a studio professor at UCLA and the Davenport Professor at Yale. His architectural designs have received numerous awards and have been exhibited in both architecture and art museums. *Time* magazine named him one of '100 Innovators for the Next Century' in 2001. He is the author of *Intricacy* (ICA, Philadelphia, 2003), *Architectural Laboratories* (NAI, 2003), *Fold, Bodies and Blobs: Collected Essays* (Exhibitions International, 1998), and *Animate Form* (Princeton Architectural Press, 1997).

Ali Rahim is an architect, associate professor at the University of Pennsylvania, visiting professor at Harvard University, and the 2007 Louis I Khan Visiting Professor at Yale. He is the co-director at Contemporary Architecture Practice, New York (www.c-a-p.net), which has established an award-winning profile in futuristic work using digital design and production techniques. Books include *Catalytic Formations: Architecture and Digital Design* (Taylor & Francis, 2005), *Contemporary Techniques in Architecture* (Wiley-Academy, 2002) and *AD Contemporary Processes in Architecture* (Wiley-Academy, 2000). Contemporary Architecture Practice's projects have been published extensively in the international press including *Der Spiegel*, the *New York Times* and the *Independent* in London. Its work has also been selected in *10x10_2* (Phaidon Press, 2005), and for *Architectural Record*'s Design Vanguard 2004 as one of 11 architectural practices worldwide 'building the future of architecture'.

Hani Rashid founded the architecture, art and design practice Asymptote with partner Lise Anne Couture in New York in 1989. Asymptote's projects include architecture, masterplanning, installation art, digital environments, and exhibition and product design. In 1996 the practice designed the Virtual Trading Floor for the New York Stock Exchange, and in 1998 a Virtual Museum for the Solomon R Guggenheim. Recently completed projects include the award-winning HydraPier in the Netherlands, Turf Club Masterplan in Penang, Malaysia, and a proposal for a new Guggenheim Museum in Guadalajara, Mexico. Projects currently being built include a commercial and cultural complex in Penang, a chapel and auditorium in the Netherlands, a masterplan for the Mexican city of Monterrey, a commercial office

tower in Budapest and luxury residential towers in Abu Dhabi and New York. Since 1989 Rashid has been an associate professor of architecture at Columbia University's Graduate School of Architecture, and is also a Professor of Architecture at the ETH, Zurich.

Joseph Rosa is the John H Bryan Curator of Architecture and Design and department chair at the Art Institute of Chicago. He is the author of numerous publications, including *Young Chicago* (Yale University Press, 2006), *Douglas Garofalo* (Yale University Press, 2006), *Next Generation Architecture* (Universe Publishing, 2003), *Folds, Blobs & Boxes: Architecture in the Digital Era* (Carnegie Museum of Art, 2001), *Albert Frey, Architecture* (Princeton Architectural Press 1990/1999), and *Louis I Kahn* (Taschen, 2006), and co-editor of *Xefirotarch/design series 4* (2006), *2 X 4/design series 3* (2005), *Glamour: Fashion, Design, Architecture* (Yale University Press, 2004), *Yves Bèhar fuseproject/ design series 2* (2004), *ROY/ design series 1* (2003), and *A Constructed View: The Architectural Photography of Julius Shulman* (Rizzoli, 1994). He is an adjunct professor at UIC and has taught at Columbia University, California College of the Arts, the University of California at Berkeley, and SCI-Arc.

Patrik Schumacher has been a designer at Zaha Hadid Architects since 1988. He is a director and senior designer of the practice, and was project architect for the 1992 Vitra Fire Station and project director for the Centre of Contemporary Art and Architecture in Rome, for the feasibility study for the new Guggenheim Museum for Taichung, Taiwan (2003), and for Soho City, a new large residential neighbourhood in Beijing. Two projects recently opened are the Ordrupgaard Museum extension in Copenhagen and the Phaeno Science Centre in Wolfsburg, Germany. He has been teaching at various architectural schools in the UK, continental Europe and the US since 1992, and is a co-director of the Design Research Laboratory at the Architectural Association School of Architecture.

Preston Scott Cohen is the Gerald M McCue Professor of Architecture and director of the Master in Architecture programmes at Harvard University Graduate School of Design. His work involves a distinctive synthesis of architectural typologies, descriptive geometries, contemporary programmes and digital media. Among his most

recognised projects are the first-prize-winning international competition design for the Tel Aviv Museum of Art (Progressive Architecture Awards Programme, 2004), the Montague House and Torus House (PA Awards in 1998 and 2000), Goodman House (2004), and the competition proposal for the Eyebeam Museum of Art and Technology in New York (2001). He is the recipient of an Academy Award in Architecture from the American Academy of Arts and Letters (2004), and author of *Contested Symmetries and Other Predicaments in Architecture* (Princeton Architectural Press, 2001) and *Permutations of Descriptive Geometry* (forthcoming). His work has been widely exhibited and published internationally and is in the collections of several museums including MoMA in New York.

Kivi Sotamaa is an assistant professor of architecture at the graduate design school of Ohio State University, visiting professor at the Universität für Angewandte Kunst, Institut für Architektur, Vienna, and the principal of SOTAMAA architecture & design. His work has been exhibited at MoMA, the Wexner Centre for the Arts, Kiasma Museum of Contemporary Art, Fondazione Trussardi and the 21st Century Museum of Contemporary Art Kanazawa. Publications featuring his work include the *New York Times*, Phaidon's *10x10 Architects*, *New Scandinavian Design*, *Forum Sweden*, *Architectural Design*, *Praxis*, *Kenhiku Bunka*, *L'Arca* and *Domus*.

J Meejin Yoon is currently an associate professor in the Department of Architecture at MIT, and founder of MY Studio. Her interdisciplinary design projects include architectural projects, interactive installations, concept clothing and artist books. MY Studio's work has been exhibited at MoMA, LA MOCA and the Cooper-Hewitt National Design Museum. Yoon's work received three Design Distinction awards from *I.D.* magazine in 2004, and has been published in *Material Process: Young Architects 4* (Princeton Architectural Press, 2003), and reviewed in the *New York Times*, *Boston Globe*, the *New Yorker*, *Financial Times*, *New York Arts Magazine*, *Architectural Lighting*, *Domus* and *Metro New York*. She was a recipient of a Fulbright Fellowship to Seoul, Korea, in 1997, received the Young Architects Award from the Architectural League of New York in 2002, and the Rome Prize Fellowship in Design from the American Academy in Rome in 2005.

CONTENTS

Epic Proportions
of Gilgamesh

Howard Watson encounters Gilgamesh, an anonymously designed north London bar. Its 'jaw-dropping ostentation' takes the unlikely form of extensive Indian relief sculptures that depict Babylonian tales at an epic scale.

Camden, the time-warped scruff of a London enclave where punk and Goth revivalism never wane amongst the warren of market stalls, tattoo parlours and cheap food stalls, now has a hulking great alien standing tall at its very heart. Dissolute, alternative adolescents, picking at earrings that might just express their idea of nonconformity, are as open-mouthed as if they had seen a Bulgari Hotel Spa in the middle of the Green Field at Glastonbury. The alien is Gilgamesh, an ultra-designed bar and restaurant, reported to cost anywhere between £12 million and £25 million, which is dragging the style cognoscenti out of the West End and single-handedly threatening to change the whole aura of Camden.

Every weekend, hundreds of thousands of people come to Camden to graze at the market stalls, but although there are a handful of half-decent bars and clubs, when the stalls shut up shop in the early evening the area becomes a litter-strewn ghost town. The mysterious owners and backers of Gilgamesh decided that the only way to force people to look at Camden as a stylish, night-time destination was to design on an epic scale, literally. The interior of the 2,500-square-metre (26,910-square-foot) venture, set within a triangular, mostly glazed building that stands above the low-level Stables Market area, is inspired by the palace in the *Epic of Gilgamesh*, which describes the adventures of the Babylonian king who battles men, gods and monsters on his journey towards enlightenment. The design is absolutely narrative, in the simplest definition of the word and, taking its cue from the shift in successful bar and restaurant design in recent years, it is consciously experiential and leans towards maximalism: like it or not, no one can leave Gilgamesh without having had a very strong sense of a 'design experience'.

Gilgamesh, Gilgamesh Design Team, Camden, London, 2006
The chairs in the restaurant are hand carved, featuring the head of Gilgamesh and his arms holding a sword handle. The curved roof is fully retractable.

The 50-metre (164-foot) bar counter divides the restaurant from the bar lounge and sets out the design's ostentatious, narrative intentions. Hand-carved friezes, above and below, tell the story of the *Epic of Gilgamesh*, while the counter top also reveals the tale through lapis lazuli tiles. Above, heating is provided by a NASA-developed radiant system, which heats the body rather than the air.

Above: It could be Vegas, it could be Disney, but Gilgamesh is saved by an exuberant attention to detail that underpins its show of historical opulence. The specially commissioned rams' heads feature detailing in lapis lazuli.
Left: No corner is left unadorned – even the DJ booth is hand carved to form part of the story. It stands between two 3-metre (10-foot) high statues bearing the head of Gilgamesh. The designers were inspired by artworks and artefacts in the British Museum.

The design itself tells the story of Gilgamesh through a series of intricately detailed friezes. The 50-metre (164-foot) U-shaped bar counter, which divides the main bar lounge from the restaurant, tells the story three times. Gilgamesh and the epic's other principal characters move from scene to scene in the form of metre-high figures picked out in bronzed relief and LED lighting against the wooden counter front. The counter top also tells the tale in exquisitely detailed lapis lazuli tiles, which makes this a likely contender for the most expensive bar counter ever seen, while a copper frieze runs above the length of one side of the bar. The heavy wood of the bar lounge is leavened by a floor-to-ceiling, curved stone frieze, which has a horizontal slit that reveals the service kitchen. Another copper frieze runs above the design's most monumental feature: two 4-metre (13-foot) high, sphinx-like statues bearing the head of Gilgamesh that stand either side of the carved wooden DJ booth.

The surprises of Gilgamesh, beyond the jaw-dropping ostentation of the storytelling, are the level of detail that has gone into the design and the consideration of the space. The huge, single floor is broken up into four distinct areas: chill

The Babylon VIP Lounge has its own circular bar counter, again with a lapis lazuli tile counter top, and bronzed friezes. Its soft furnishings, embroidered with golden thread, suggest even greater opulence than those in the main lounge bar.

bar, lounge bar, restaurant and VIP lounge and, within the spaces, slight variations in level and furnishings resist monotony and repetition. The positioning of the fixtures and the carved furnishings also help divide the space, offering a sense of intimacy. The owners claim that the carvings are the work of 10,000 North Indian craftsmen. Much about Gilgamesh carries a suitable aura of the mysterious and apocryphal – almost every element is described along the lines of 'the longest in Europe' or 'the best in Britain', while the designers remain strictly anonymous.

But when one considers that every single chair is hand carved with a slightly individual design, the exaggeration stops seeming quite so ridiculous. Almost all the furniture is in dark, heavy wood sourced from India and is carved to extend the tale of Gilgamesh. Most notably, the curved banquettes in the bars have their own section of the story on the back, ensuring that there is no dead space in the design. The restaurant chairs, deliberately wide to give the sense of a throne, have finials in the form of the face of Gilgamesh, while the arms are his extended forearms, holding the handle of a sword which points downwards to become the chair leg. The hugely expensive carved-stone frieze extends into an area no one will ever see, while the service doors and air conditioning are totally disguised within the fretwork.

The fear is that this re-creation of another world could be a Disneyland or Las Vegas experience, where superficiality and crassness continually weaken the credulousness of the narrative. Gilgamesh is never going to appeal to everybody, but the detail of its design execution, in a deliberate attempt to offer a uniquely experiential, luxurious space, must be applauded. Interestingly, though, where the real world cannot be shut out, it is embraced by the design. Surrounding all these dark woods and heavy materials are walls of floor-to-ceiling glazing, much of which looks onto the surrounding market. However, along the side of the restaurant and Babylon VIP Lounge is a rail track, just a few metres away and at the same height as the diners. Intermittingly, a huge train will (almost silently) pass along the length of the exterior – the designers chose to leave the glazing completely naked to make the most of this surprising, filmic happening.

In terms of media hype, Gilgamesh has succeeded because the epic has been matched by the detail, making it more than a one-trick pony. Camden is responding – property developers have heard the Gilgamesh tills ringing and plans are afoot for further design-led enterprises. However, the renaissance may turn out to be a threat to the market culture that gives Camden its particular charm. ∆

Howard Watson is a London-based writer and editor. He is the author of *The Design Mix: Bars, Cocktails & Style*, *Hotel Revolution: 21st-Century Hotel Design*, and *Bar Style: Hotels and Members' Clubs*, all published by John Wiley & Sons.

Weiss/Manfredi
Architects

For at least a decade, Weiss/Manfredi Architects has been considered one of the top New York firms – contenders for prestigious public commissions that require more than a good solid commercial job. Now, with the opening of the Seattle Art Museum's Olympic Sculpture Park, they are making their mark on the national scene in the US, and their particular talent for place making is being widely recognised. **Jayne Merkel** talks with partners Marion Weiss and Michael Manfredi about that talent and how it developed.

Competitions, which are relatively rare in the US, can give young architects the opportunity to show what they can do long before they receive the kinds of commission that would otherwise make that possible. But for husband and wife team Marion Weiss and Michael Manfredi, early success in competitions even determined the direction their practice would take.

Their work encompasses landscape as well as built form, partly because the first major commission they won, for the Women's Memorial and Education Center at Arlington National Cemetery, Washington DC, is built within the cemetery grounds and thus visually connected with them. The partially submerged, glass-walled structure is carved into the land behind a historic (but neglected) hemispherical entry arch designed by McKim, Mead & White. A glass ceiling with texts etched into its surface allows changes in the weather to be seen and sensed inside just as they are in the landscape while at the same time honouring the veterans. The awe-inspiring cemetery grounds are ever present in the elegant, dignified pavilion, commissioned in 1989 and completed in 1997, where the stories of the more than two million women who have served their country, from the revolutionary war to the present, are told on the hallowed ground that had previously been thought to commemorate only male soldiers. This inside-outside connection allows these women to join their countrymen but still have a place of their own – one with a view across the Potomac River and of the seat of government of the nation they helped defend.

Weiss notes that her firm's propensity to meld architecture and landscape was not simply a matter of luck: 'We entered the competitions that led us in that direction because the questions they asked were broad.' She goes on to say that the current, narrow definition of architecture may be what is unusual: Historically, architects did everything from infrastructure for bridges to vestments for the Vatican. The terrain of design was not as administratively bifurcated as it is today.'

Also, both partners have a long-standing interest in landscape. As Manfredi notes: 'Marion grew up in California in an area with apricot orchards. Her backyard was a Jesuit retreat with streams. And I grew up in the hills of Rome. I remember distinctly playing in the Villa Giulia. I can't remember whether it was the garden or the villa, but now the two are inseparable in the mind. From those very different trajectories, we gravitated towards this common interest.'

Weiss and Manfredi met whilst working in the office of Mitchell Giurgola in New York, where Romaldo Giurgola, who had been a student of Louis I Kahn and taught the history of the Italian Renaissance, reinforced their tendency to see architecture as inextricably connected to the land. The partners say they have always been 'drawn to sites where the act of construction clarifies distinct aspects of a setting,

Women's Memorial and Education Center, Arlington National Cemetery, Washington DC, 1997
Views into the centre from Arlington Memorial Cemetery – and out on to the cemetery from inside – through the angular glass ceiling make the women's histories part of the larger national narrative.

whether that setting is a room, a city or an unobstructed landscape'. What they do not say is that their projects have a delicacy and quality of detail that reinforces the clarification.

An early project, the Olympia Fields Park and Community Center in South Chicago, Illinois, completed in 1996, connects an existing 4-hectare (10-acre) park with a nursery about the same size and incorporates a number of 19th-century farm buildings. These simple white-painted wood structures inspired an arc-shaped, milled wood trellis that defines a major outdoor space that is excavated in a series of terraces for water retention purposes. The excavation gives the otherwise flat landscape an aspect of architectural form, and the delicate open trellis recalls trees in a landscape. The park also has a new pond for flood prevention, and a working windmill that is part of the irrigation system (as well as, now, a landmark for the community). Landscape and architecture overlap at several points.

Building and landscape merge even more intensely in the Museum of the Earth, a new museum for the Paleontological Research Institution in Ithaca, New York, completed in 2004. The commission was tailormade for the practice, not only because the subject matter of the museum came from the earth (it houses one of the nation's largest collections of paleontological artefacts) and occupies a dramatic hillside site overlooking Lake Cayuga, but also because Manfredi, who went to school in Ithaca at Cornell, had done some studies on the geological forces that shaped the gorges there. In addition, Weiss's mother was a geologist so as a child she hiked around

---

Museum of the Earth, Paleontological Research Institution, Ithaca, New York, 2004
With fissures in the structure of the Museum of the Earth above ground, where it splits into two parts, the building echoes the geology of the gorges in the hilly, northern New York State college town where it is located. Stepping down the hillside also provides dramatic views of the topology.

Smith College Campus Center, Northampton, Massachusetts, 2003

Located at the centre of the campus, the student centre mediates between dormitories and classroom buildings while providing a place for students, faculty and staff to socialise informally. The building is defined by a series of interconnecting paths that converge on a long, curved skylit gallery, blurring the distinction between inside and outside.

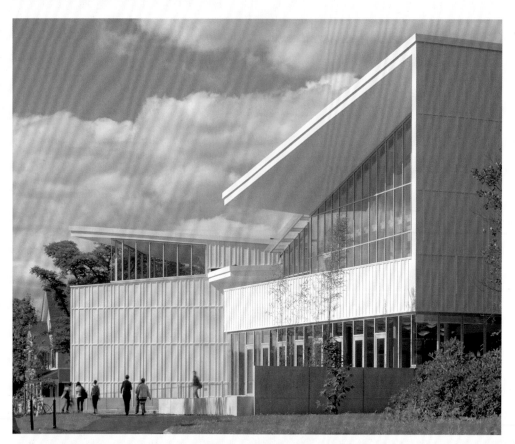

Barnard College Nexus arts centre, Barnard College, Columbia University, New York, due for completion 2008

The architects have designed this enclosed urban building as a transparent and translucent box with the studios, theatres, café spaces and classrooms connected by a series of slipped atria. The building also mediates two levels of the campus with a series of landscaped terraces, framing a clear site line from the entrance gates on Broadway to the historic core. Views through the building and campus are linked vertically through ascending atria that bring landscape and light into the heart of the building.

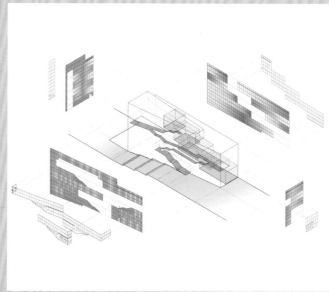

on difficult terrain with her family to study the earth. 'The director of the museum was passionate about paleontology, which he viewed as a marriage of biology and geology, and that's what is interesting to us – things like how do you do water management – which are usually seen as civil engineering issues,' Weiss explains.

The museum, cut into a hillside overlooking the lake and adjacent to an existing building, is organised as two parallel, interconnected buildings. Below ground, an interactive research gallery links the buildings, and is supported by a clear span structure that will accommodate expansion in the future. Together, the two buildings define the edges of a cascading plaza with views of the lake.

The architects' approach lends itself to projects where building and landscape merge. 'Marion and I started mostly by drawing sections and multiple perspectives. This serial quality was something we were very interested in pushing,' says Manfredi. And Weiss continues: 'Architecture is experienced through movement. We like the temporal qualities in a work. Because all the projects are driven by sections, there is a route up, down or around. The Museum of the Earth burrows into a hill. Smith insinuates itself into a built-up campus. Barnard moves vertically to claim its territory in a hyper-urban situation.'

The route seems more horizontal in the 5,574-square-metre (60,000-square-foot) student centre the architects designed for the verdant, largely Victorian campus of Smith College in the quaint small town of Northampton, Massachusetts, because the ground is relatively flat. But movement inside goes up, down and around because the site, next to an historic auditorium on a little slice of land, was not really large enough to accommodate all the required spaces, thus the building twists through the site like a snake. It also had to mediate between Elm Street, a major street in the town, and a big campus oval that had been planned by the Olmsted Brothers but never completed.

Here, the architects developed a building with a chameleon section that winds around the edge of the auditorium, moving in plan from the slender face of Elm Street and unfurling into a broad glass expanse on the great lawn of Chapin Oval. They threaded the landscape through the glass, steel and wood building, which has a series of outdoor terraces connecting the dining areas and lounges with the campus grounds. And, as at Olympia Fields, the architecture itself reflects its context. Wood batons and wood plywood sheets superimposed on a double-wall subframe and painted white give the building texture in a modern version of traditional American small-town architecture (though most of the Smith campus itself is brick, many of its residential buildings are wood).

At a new 9,290-square-metre (100,000-square-foot) 'Nexus' arts building for Barnard College, the women's college at Columbia University in Manhattan, the organisational path moves up and around in a vertical, angular pattern. Weiss/Manfredi's scheme, selected in a national competition in 2003, actually uses less land than was allocated for the building in a masterplan by Hardy Holzman Pfeiffer because

Olympia Fields Park and Community Center, South Chicago, Illinois, 1996
This design for a new park preserves the character of the 19th-century farm and nursery that stood on the property, while providing a sustainable flood prevention and irrigation system.

the facilities are stacked vertically and linked diagonally so that all the different areas are visible from one another and the rest of the campus. Thus students and staff can see the painting and architecture studios, performance spaces, black box theatre, café, reading room, seminar areas and classrooms as they move through the building or around the campus. 'The vertical dimension is engaged by a lateral cut through the building that is accomplished through a series of slipped atria,' Manfredi explains.

Views into the various spaces are provided by three types of glass with differing degrees of transparency. One is opaque with ceramic fritting, and there are translucent versions that modulate the transparency of the building with coloured acid-edged fritting of varying degrees. There is acid-edged colour integral glass, which is even more translucent. And there is clear glass. 'So it's a gradient,' Weiss points out. 'We also have a gradient of translucency and transparency and of colour that is calibrated across the building to correspond to the programme.' The translucent terracotta colour translates the nearby Columbia and Barnard buildings into a contemporary language. Bathrooms, of course, are opaque, public areas are transparent, and studios have appropriate natural light.

The challenge in Seattle was almost the opposite of that at Barnard. Instead of an intensely developed site, the Olympic Sculpture Park occupies a 3.4-hectare (8.5-acre), hilly, derelict area where railway tracks and a highway had cut the waterfront off from the city. Again the architects used a chameleon section 'that is sometimes a building, sometimes an earthwork, and sometimes a bridge' to connect the edge of downtown to Puget Sound, the body of the water between

Olympic Sculpture Park, Seattle Art Museum, Seattle, Washington, 2006

This urban sculpture park on the site of a former fuel-storage and transfer facility creates a connection between the downtown and the waterfront, which are separated by railway tracks and a highway. Visitors enter a glass-enclosed exhibition pavilion with performance space and educational facilities and follow a Z-shaped path that links a range of works of art along the way, culminating in the shoreline with its newly restored aquatic life.

Seattle and the Pacific Ocean, 12 metres (40 feet) below, by means of a wide and dramatic angled Z-shaped green platform. 'This revels in the fact that it's an artificial landscape,' Weiss explains. 'It doesn't pretend to be anything else.'

The angled path links a delicate transparent exhibition pavilion at the top of the park, which becomes a beacon at night, with the waterfront. Along the way, it connects three archetypal Northwest landscapes – a dense evergreen forest, lush woods of deciduous trees, and a shoreline garden of low-lying pines and aquatic terraces with kelp, algae and grasses to attract fish. Visitors will also encounter artist-designed infrastructure projects, such as pedestrian bridges and benches, as well as anchor works, such as Richard Serra's 23-metre (75-foot) long *Wake* and Mark Dion's *Vivarium*, along with temporary exhibitions, all of which will be framed by views of Elliot Bay, the city skyline and Mount Ranier.

The project, begun in 2001 and opened on 28 October 2006, tries to break down the usual cultural barriers between the art precinct and the rest of the city. It is part park, part museum, part connective tissue – building, landscape, cityscape and new kind of place. And it has earned Weiss/Manfredi a unique reputation. They were the only American architects included in 'Groundswell: Constructing the Contemporary Landscape', the Museum of Modern Art's 2005 exhibition about 'how designers and urban planners are reclaiming formerly obsolete and degraded sites for public spaces'. They are certain to be considered for other commissions, like this, of unique kinds. ⌂

Resumé

Weiss/Manfredi Architects

1989
Weiss/Manfredi Architects founded in New York
Women's Memorial and Education Center, Arlington National Cemetery, Washington DC, competition (first prize)

1992
Olympia Fields Park and Community Center, South Chicago, Illinois, international competition (first prize)

1993
Bridging the Gaps international competition (first place)

1996
Olympia Fields Park and Community Center completed

1997
Selected as an 'Emerging Voice' by the Architectural League of New York
Women's Memorial and Education Center completed
Winner of the ID Magazine Environments Annual Design Award: Olympia Fields Park and Community Center

1999
Winner of ID Magazine's Environments Annual Design Award: Women's Memorial and Education Center

2000
Museum of the Earth and Women's Memorial exhibited at 'Design Culture Now: National Design Triennial, Cooper-Hewitt, National Design Museum, New York

2001
Olympic Sculpture Park, Seattle Art Museum, international competition (first prize)

2002
'Reflect/Remember, a post 9/11 manifesto' exhibited in 'A New World Trade Center: Design Proposals', Venice Architecture Biennale, Venice, Italy
National AIA Honor Awards: Women's Memorial and Education Center and Olympia Fields Park

2003
NYC 2012 Olympic Rowing Venues at Flushing Meadows Corona Park exhibited in 'Metropolis, New York', V BIA – São Paolo International Biennial of Architecture and Design, São Paolo, Brazil
Barnard College Nexus, invited competition for mixed-use arts centre in Manhattan, New York (first prize) – due for completion 2008

Progressive Architecture Award: Olympic Sculpture Park, Seattle Art Museum

2004
Academy Award for Architecture, American Academy of Arts and Letters
New York AIA Excellence in Design Award: Museum of the Earth

2005
Olympic Sculpture Park exhibited at 'Groundswell: Designing the Contemporary Landscape', Museum of Modern Art, New York
New York AIA Projects Honor Award: Barnard College Nexus,
New York AIA Architecture Honor Award: Smith College Campus Center

2006
Venice Biennale: US Exhibition featuring University of Penn Studio 'Resilient Topographies'
Olympic Sculpture Park completed

Marion Weiss

Michael Manfredi

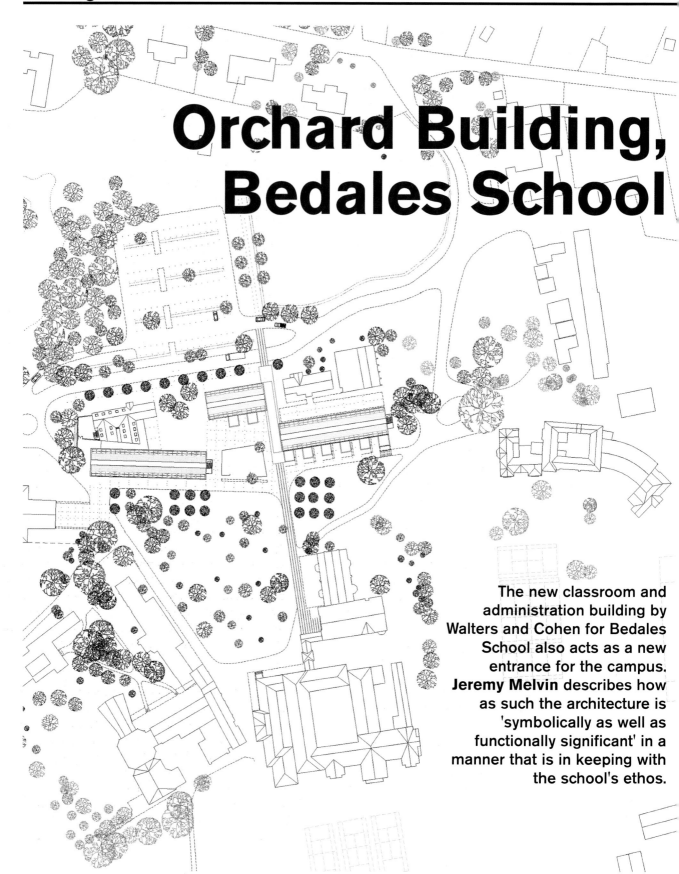

Orchard Building, Bedales School

The new classroom and administration building by Walters and Cohen for Bedales School also acts as a new entrance for the campus. **Jeremy Melvin** describes how as such the architecture is 'symbolically as well as functionally significant' in a manner that is in keeping with the school's ethos.

Larch-clad and metal-roofed, the Orchard Building brings varied textures and finishes to its rational and precise forms.

The building is part of an important route within the school grounds

In making the mental condition of the building worker a central element in architectural thought, Ruskin set one of the preconditions for later writers to put forward all manner of relationships between architecture and education. Buildings did not just provide space for teaching, but could also themselves teach, and part of what they taught comprised the spiritual and emotional insights of past generations, tying the ideas of 'spirit' and individual well-being into a didactic framework. Among the numerous iterations and manifestations of this are the early women's colleges at Oxford and Cambridge, the London board schools and CR Ashbee's Guild of Handicraft in Chipping Camden, to say nothing of Ruskin's own educational forays. Most deserved one or other meaning of the term 'progressive', and Walters and Cohen's Orchard Building for Bedales School shows how this tradition can be updated in a contemporary idiom.

Bedales has been at the forefront of progressive education for over a hundred years. Its founder, John Haden Badley, was steeped in Ruskinian thought even before he heard Ruskin's last Slade lecture at Oxford in 1884, so the ageing magus's analogy between the 'condition of England' and a fat pig on that occasion was not alone responsible for Badley's determination to found a school where handwork

and brainwork, outdoor and indoor activities flowed into each other as part of the educational experience.

To explain why the school picked Walters and Cohen for the new Orchard Building, the present headmaster, Keith Budge, sitting on a Barnsley-designed chair, delves into the school's ethos. From the start Badley saw the presence of beauty as an important adjunct to teaching and learning because it could enrich and strengthen those experiences. But it was beauty of a practical, Arts and Crafts sort – 'new chairs are more comfortable than these', he confides – but there can be no finer demonstration of the Arts and Crafts belief in aligning hand- and brainwork than the library, designed in 1921 by Ernest Gimson as a memorial to old Bedaleans who died in the First World War. Its interior, at least, shows how a Cotswold barn can be reinterpreted as a library, with pegged timber trusses, wide floor boards and semiprivate alcoves where students can enjoy the wide and erudite collection.

Beauty's role in the school is also apparent in the 'aesthetics committee' which ensures a consistent approach across the entire estate, where all interventions have to work from the prescribed palette of materials. Underlying this policy is a belief made explicit in the buildings themselves; that every element of the estate has to play a part in the students'

Walters and Cohen, Orchard Building, Bedales School, Petersfield, Guildford, 2005
Site plan. Bedales has 53 hectares (130 acres) of grounds, park and farmland, with a group of buildings of varying ages. The Orchard Building is the two ranges on either side of the spine leading from the car park to the main quad. Also shown is a later phase, to the left between the Orchard Building and the theatre.

A top-floor classroom, where the steeply pitched roof enhances the room's spatial qualities.

Detail section. The cross-section is the key to the design. It is essentially simple construction, but angled and placed to gain the maximum from each component and 'free' energy to reduce running costs and improve the quality of the environment. A small room off the access gallery is shown in elevation.

experience of the school. This includes the traditional farm buildings and barns the students have reconstructed which now serve as bakeries and smithies for 'outdoor' work.

But for a school that charges fees of almost £25,000 a year, the classroom is all-important. Early on, remembers Budge, Cindy Walters stressed the importance of sensible orientation, good daylight and effective ventilation in decent classrooms, drawing on her firm's experience in the state sector and in particular their proposals for the DfES Schools for the Future initiative, where they worked with the environmental engineer Max Fordham. All this sounded very appropriate for the classroom and administration building that was to replace long-serving prefabricated sheds, and in a neat echo of Ruskin's preference for 'spirit' over outward form, Walters and Cohen's insistence on the marriage of subliminal and functional aspects of classroom design overcame any discrepancy between Arts and Crafts architecture and their own.

What brought this initial potential to fruition was the effective working structure established by the school. After appointing an architect governor – Edward Williams of Hopkins Architects, an old Bedalean and contemporary of Walters and Cohen – Bedales established a committee to oversee the project which, housing 60 per cent of the school's classrooms and in effect an entrance to its campus, was symbolically as well as functionally significant. As the first phase of a masterplan it would also set the tone for the school's ongoing evolution. It fell to a specially constituted subcommittee to draw out the compatibility between the architects' and

school's visions of what a classroom should be, and how it could be at the centre of a total experience of school, which in Badley's formulation comprised 'head, heart and spirit'.

Walters and Cohen's work for the DfES helped to establish a number of generic forms for classrooms as well as layouts for schools. Light and ventilation were crucial for the former, while schools, they argued, could benefit from combining communal with circulation space. The Orchard Building adapts these for the context of Bedales in several ways. First, i has to conform to local planning regulations that stipulate 'two floors and a roof', a departure from the normal DfES guidelines of single-storey schools, which are not immediately conducive to educational needs. Walters and Cohen managed to turn this to their advantage. Picking up on the relatively steep pitch of 55 degrees that occurs on several of Bedales' buildings, they found that a full classroom could be inserted into the attic storey. What might be lost in width is made up in the extra height, with the benefits of light, view and air. The architects also introduced vertical shafts between floors, adding to the spatial richness and helping to bring an intensity to the sense of community that a spreading, single-storey building could not achieve. Modern languages on the top floor, maths on the first and English on the ground are all related elements within a complex whole.

How the design fosters a very particular notion of community is a second adaptation of the DfES studies. Bedales prides itself on being a homogeneous community where the hierarchies of traditional public schools do not

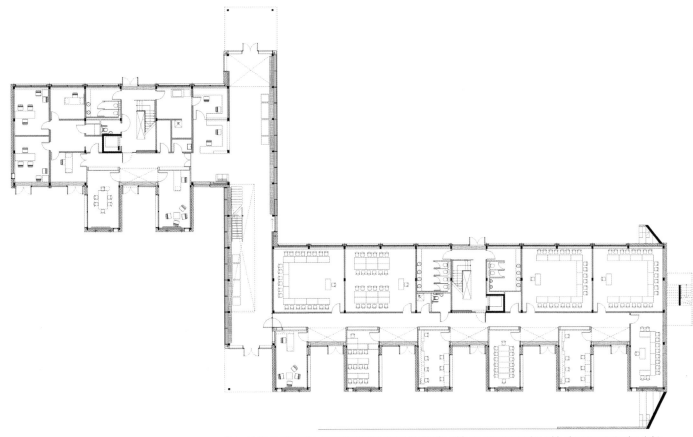

Ground-floor plan. The general arrangement is simple, with an entrance spine with classrooms to the right and staff offices to the left. Classrooms on the upper floors follow a similar configuration.

The top-floor gallery, where students can congregate informally or work individually on small tables alongside smaller rooms where staff can see students privately.

A hallmark of Walters and Cohen's work is to extract aesthetic effect from simple components and forms.

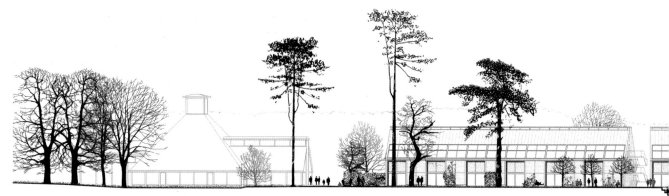

Section AA. Long section through the Orchard Building, showing Feilden Clegg's theatre, completed in 1997 – another building with 55-degree roof pitch.

Section BB. Long section with the theatre to the right.

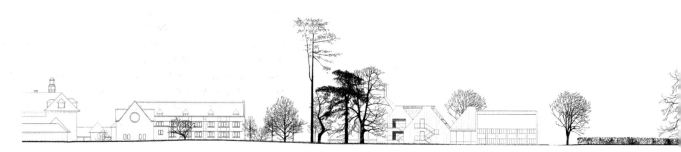

Section CC. Site section showing Gimson's library in the elevation to the left of the Orchard Building.

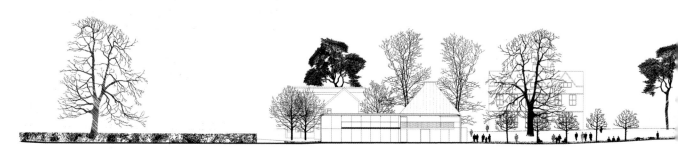

Section DD. Site section.

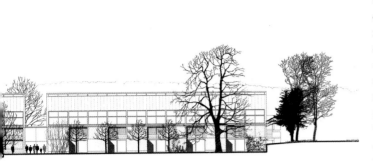

exist: dress is informal, students are on first-name terms with teachers and, after assembly, they all shake hands with each other. This helps to set the tone for a society where relationships with others segue into various stimuli that come from the physical environment to encourage and enhance learning. In Bedales' parkland setting, the physical environment starts with nature, which the students experience directly with outdoor work, before the buildings gradually introduce an element of intellectual control into the environment, which finally reaches its apotheosis in the actual moment of education – that almost theatrical instant where intellectual content, setting and communication between student and teacher seem to merge.

The architects' task was to create an environment where this can happen. The classrooms are relatively conventional in form as this allows for more flexibility. English teachers, for example, prefer a U-shape layout of desks, while mathematicians favour rows facing forward and, as Budge points out, with a life of a good 50 years any pandering to currently fashionable educational ideas would circumscribe future developments. With this in mind they are all wired for IT, but also have shelf space for textbooks. Students will probably appreciate the classroom design subliminally; with better light and ventilation than usual they should be less strained and fatigued.

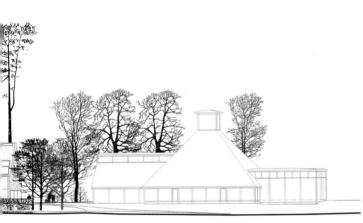

Outside the classrooms the learning experience continues in a less formal way. Wide access galleries and the vertical shafts mean staff and students can see many of their colleagues and fellow students, while there is also space for desks and small meeting tables for casual chats and private study – all of them in a wireless-enabled Internet access zone. Across the galleries from the classrooms are smaller rooms for individual or small group teaching. In this dynamic between casual and formal contact, the sense of community evolves in line with the personal development of education.

A final element of the design is the way it contributes to the school's sense of identity. A high porch clearly marks an entrance that leads to the reception area, conceived as an internal piazza with views one way to the senior staff offices, straight ahead towards the rest of the school and upwards to the classrooms. It feels like the hub of the community and the detailed design reinforces this sense. Rather than mimic Gimson's luscious Arts and Crafts detailing, in the Orchard Building Walters and Cohen use modern means to achieve a similarly satisfying economy, such as the slender columns that suspend the first-floor gallery over the entrance, worked out with structural engineers Adams Kara Taylor. The basic form, with two storeys and a 55-degree roof pitch, echoes other buildings, but again, with larch cladding, does not replicate them. In them something new seems to emerge from a living tradition, and that in itself could be a metaphor for the sort of education Bedales seeks to offer. ∆

New River Village

Social affordable housing is so often the poor relation of any private development, allocated the poorest plot with the least attractive aspect. **Bruce Stewart** describes how at Hornsey in north London, Stock Woolstencroft has transcended these problems with considerate spatial organisation and security management

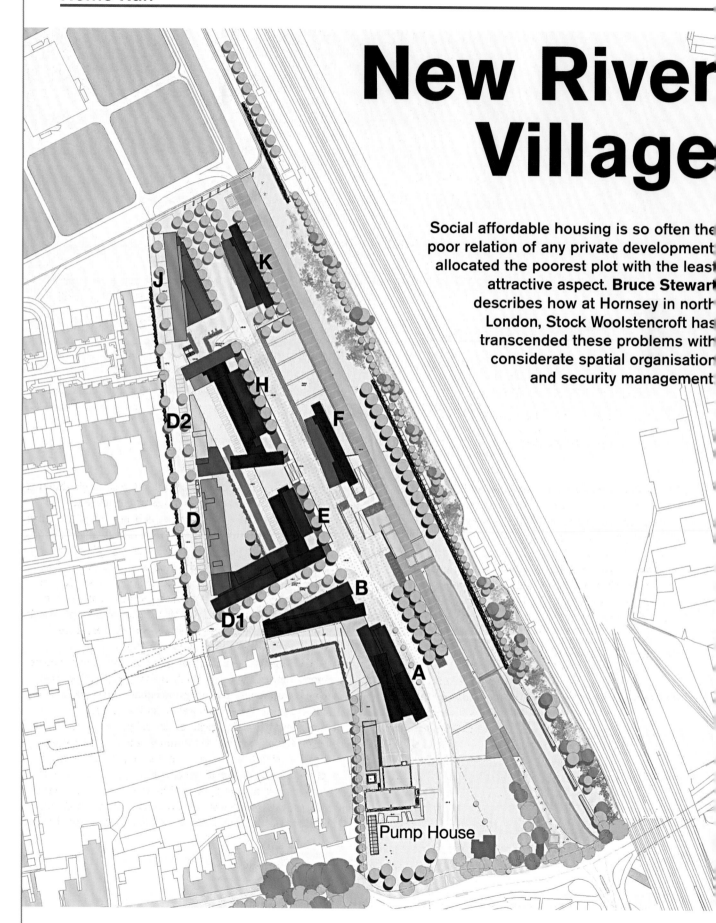

Pump House

Stock Woolstencroft, New River Village, Hornsey, Haringey, London, 2000–08
The fall of 8 metres (26 feet) across the site means that the rental block D is at a lower level than the private-sector block it faces internally. This level change differentiates the blocks spatially, but does not alienate the affordable element visually.

Situated in the north London borough of Haringey, New River Village is one of the area's largest, recent, new residential developments. Lying in the shadow of Alexandra Palace, the development is in the district known as Hornsey – a once thriving Edwardian suburb that echoes its counterparts elsewhere in London architecturally, but has not always maintained the well-to-do, middle-class resident base prevalent in such areas as west London. However, this is changing. The currently more affluent 'villages' bordering Hornsey, such as Crouch End and Muswell Hill, are boosting property prices in the area and making the locale much more attractive to prospective residents. And it is this economic environment that has encouraged property developers St James to undertake the construction of the more than 600 apartments and commercial space that make up New River Village.

The site is on land previously owned by Thames Water Authority and used for the treatment of part of London's water supply. In fact, the area has a long history of involvement with the supply of water to the city, the New River itself being constructed in 1613 as the first of the external water supplies needed to support a rapidly growing London. Resembling a shallow canal, the river has gradually

been neglected and forms a vital part of the strategic thinking by the architects of the new project, Stock Woolstencroft.

The London-based practice was established in 1989 and has a great deal of experience in most fields of architecture, but particular strengths in housing and urban renewal/regeneration. Having worked very closely with several governmental bodies – both local and national – and several housing associations, the architects' knowledge of the problems currently facing house builders is extensive, and they have won several awards for their work on housing projects, including a Housing Design Award for New River Village in 2005.

While Stock Woolstencroft may not be perceived as one of London's more esoteric or overtly theoretical practices, they bring a commitment to quality and equality that many architectural firms could do well to look at. Their commitment to viewing each residential project as an opportunity for the wider community or a particular site, rather than simply an insertion in the city, makes for a carefully balanced approach to design.

The original planning proposal for the site, by a different developer, was for a much lower-density project of 142 units – low-rise brick-clad houses and apartments – of the quality and

Site plan showing the organisation of the buildings across it. The blocks containing the affordable units (D, D2 and J) are to the west of the site. While this slightly removes them from the New River itself, they enjoy good sunlight and views up to Alexandra Palace which is to the north. As part of the strategy for opening the site up to the wider community of Hornsey, both banks of the river have been redeveloped with new planting and walkways.

While the affordable/social housing elements are less ornate than the private-sector blocks, there is a consistency in the architectural language used.

design more associated with provincial housing developments constructed during the 1980s. The outline proposal also included a large supermarket and all of the parking that this would require. However, when the scheme was given to Stock Woolstencroft, they quickly saw the potential of the site not only in terms of increased density, but also in the benefits that could be provided for the wider local community – for example, the provision of open space to provide secure pedestrian routes through the site. As a result they submitted a proposal for a density of 449 units (this is currently being uplifted to 629 units, giving a density of 485 units/hectare).

The site's position, along the western bank of the New River on Hornsey High Street, placed it at the centre of a much wider redevelopment project being backed by the local borough. This zone, known as the 'Haringey Heartlands', is key for the regeneration of the postindustrial landscape that covers much of north London. With this in mind, the overall site strategy was therefore to not only build homes for the private and public sectors, but to reinvest in the wider community by providing a large amount of open green space along both banks of the waterway (and not just the one that borders the site). The new green space will therefore be overlooked by some of the private housing blocks, but will be open to the general public at all times. Such open access can often create security issues – for both property and individuals – but by employing the 'Secure by Design' guidelines (a governmental initiative to encourage developers and architects to design housing that actively reduces the possibility of crime), the architects have ensured that there are no hidden or secluded spots in the park, and the proximity of well-illuminated paths and buildings will add a self-policing element.

In addition to the green space, the overall site strategy also included the refurbishment of a listed Edwardian pumping station to create a large restaurant and gallery space, which is now run in conjunction with the Royal Academy, which has a resident artist in place.

The social/affordable element of the development is placed to the west of the site away from the river. While this does slightly distance these units from the new green space, it does not mean that they are in a significantly poorer quality area. West-facing, they enjoy good summer sun and have excellent views towards Alexandra Palace. Unusually, two housing associations are involved in the development. Circle Anglian manages the rented flats in block D1, and the Metropolitan Housing Trust (MHT) blocks D and D2. Block J, which has some rented accommodation with individual access on the ground floor, the rest being shared-ownership flats, is co-managed by both. These four blocks of affordable housing provide 188 units in total and constitute 29 per cent of the total scheme.

This arrangement of two registered social landlords (RSLs) has led to a slight variation in the appearance of the separately managed blocks – for example, the units managed by MHT have a more austere look – due to the different budgets and visions of each. However, with a single architectural practice designing the entire scheme there is a continuity of language that ensures the quality of the buildings is not compromised. Indeed, since the whole scheme is navigable by all the residents, and the wider community via the pedestrian routes through the site, it was important that the standard of the architecture remained consistent. Using inferior techniques for the affordable elements could have had a negative effect on the commercial blocks, resulting in either reduced sales prices or a much slower uptake of the private units.

There are, of course, the now familiar reasons for the social/affordable elements of the scheme being separated from the private, those of easier building management and the need for different space requirements. However, with block J in particular, the architects have managed not only to create a coherent overall development, but also shared-ownership flats that are of a very high standard in terms of internal finishes and space (though the bathrooms do tend towards the average with regard to fittings). All of the apartments have balconies which let in large amount of natural light, and those to the

NEW RIVER VILLAGE	G 0-29%	F 30-39%	E 40%	D 41-49%	C 50-59%	B 60-69%	A 70-100%
QUALITATIVE							
Space-Interior						B	
Space-Exterior							A
Location							A
Community							A
QUANTITATIVE							
Construction Cost					C		
Cost-rental/purchase					C		
Cost in use				D			
Sustainability					C		
AESTHETICS							
Good Design?							A
Appeal							A
Innovative?					C		

This table is based on an analytical method of success in contributing to a solution to housing need. The criteria are: Quality of life – does the project maintain or improve good basic standards? Quantitative factors – has the budget achieved the best it can? Aesthetics – does the building work visually?

Block J, the most northern of the buildings on the site, contains the units available for shared ownership. While all the apartments are single aspect, the ample glazing and use of balconies ensure that each unit has plenty of natural light and interesting views out over the site to the city beyond.

north of the block have wonderful views up to Alexandra Palace and the park that surrounds it.

Unfortunately, one criticism of the project is that the architects' use of often difficult geometries for all the blocks has led to some awkward layouts for individual apartments, with long dog-leg internal corridors from which the rooms lead off. Conversely, these geometries have created some leftover spaces that now provide very useful storage.

While the shared-ownership units have balconies, the rented units have garden spaces. The family houses have their own individual gardens, which vary in size due to the difficult geometries, and the rented flats share a larger open space. The gardens are internal to the main western block that combines both the rented elements and some of the private accommodation. Due to the 8-metre (26-foot) fall across the site from east to west, these spaces are overlooked by the remaining private-sector flats, which could have created a difficult situation in terms of an 'us and them' separation. However, the architecture is used to integrate the differing tenures even more successfully than they already are from the

outside, though some features do highlight the difference between the two resident groups – there is secure underground parking for the private-sector units while the residents of the housing associations have only street parking, and a private gym that is only available to private-sector residents.

Overall, New River Village is a successful project that takes on board the spatial and management differences of the two ends of the housing market, and integrates them into a coherent development using a consistent architectural language to create a well-balanced scheme that is not only reusing a large brownfield site, but also creating open space and amenities for the wider local community. ⚙

Bruce Stewart is currently researching and writing *The Architects' Navigation Guide to New Housing*, to be published in early 2007 by Wiley-Academy. He trained as an architect and is currently a college teacher at the Bartlett School of Architecture, UCL London.

McLean's Nuggets

Aeroelasticity

Aeroelasticity has been defined as 'the mutual interaction ... of inertial, elastic and aerodynamic forces'.[1] More simply, it may be described as the interaction between solid and fluid in a dynamic environment. The adverse aeroelastic effects that occur in plane wings during flight are widely studied, but it is the active control of such forces that are currently the focus of several academic and industrial research programmes. The Active Aeroelastic Wing (AAW) programme is a joint venture between the US Airforce, Boeing Phantom Works and NASA Dryden. 'AAW Research could enable thinner, higher aspect-ratio wings on future aircraft, which could result in reduced aerodynamic drag, allowing greater range or payload and improved fuel efficiency.'[2] In 2003, NASA completed the first phase of testing using a modified Boeing F/A-18, which neatly coincided with the centennial of Orville and Wilbur Wright's first powered flight. The AAW design obviates the need for separate mechanical flaps and ailerons, as did the Wright brothers' wing design with its aerodynamic properties being changed through a gentle twist, or 'wing-warping'. At the University of Bristol, on their Morphing Aircraft project,[3] through the use of a new composite wing construction of multi-axis, multilayered substrates it will be possible to twist and form a single structural entity rather than build a stable (fixed) design with additional moving parts. Bi-stable and multistable surfaces are being tested which can attain 'multiple states of equilibrium' to control 'leading edge and trailing edge deflection'.[4] One method also being explored for AAW is the use of AAW control surfaces as 'tabs' that promote wing twist. Tabs, or mini flaps, across the wing surface would, when activated, cause a local aerodynamic force, pushing or pulling the wing into the required geometry. This 'trim-tab' effect was eloquently described and analogised by Richard Buckminster Fuller in *New Forms Vs Reforms, Letter to the World Architectural Students, 1963*.[5] The movement of huge rudders and thus the direction of large passenger ships (and analogically our environment) can be activated by a much smaller secondary entity, the 'trim tab'.

Insect wing showing bio-actuator control veins.

Hidden Persuaders – The Technology of Selling

'Every time some jerk in a white coat with a stethoscope hanging around his neck holds up some toothpaste or a pack of cigarettes or a bottle of beer or a mouthwash or a jar of shampoo or a little box of something that makes a fat wrestler smell like mountain lilac I always make a note never to buy any.'
Raymond Chandler, *The Long Goodbye*, 1953

There seems no more developed an art than that of the art of selling. A kind of high art, no good business for no good reason, which develops brand conscientiousness, loyalty and associated projected lifestyle. The fact that Unilever and Proctor & Gamble manufacture a majority of the UK's soap-powder brands does not stop the industry endlessly trying to differentiate these essentially clone products by inventing and presenting product-specific unique selling points (USPs). Take Radion clothes detergent, launched with much fanfare in 1987 by insinuating that up until that point, while previous clothes washing detergents may have actually cleaned your clothes, they did not get rid of the smell ... mmm nasty, but nice. So what happened to Radion? While it immediately grabbed 2 per cent of the lucrative market (Mintel Consumer Goods report, January 2002), its sales failed to grow, so in 1997 Unilever tried a new type of campaign for the relaunch utilising 'ambient media', and the scented bus ticket was born, perhaps to remind passengers that while their well-laundered Monday work clothes were clean, they were not perhaps Radion clean. This kind of campaign approach is now widespread and includes viral marketing, guerilla marketing, and ambush marketing utilising the logic of the cultural gene, or 'Meme', first described by

Professor Richard Dawkins in his 1976 book *The Selfish Gene*. Ad (event) agencies such as the perfectly misconstruable Cunning Stunts (now soberly retitled Cunning Communications), make it their business to seed new products or services in the minds of us eminently gullible or persuadable consumers. Vance Packard (1914–96), author of the *Hidden Persuaders* (1957), was alarmed at how the technology of selling, utilising the 'pop' psychology of motivational research, was being extended into politics and thus government. His critics derided him as essentially a moralist, but his dissection of psychosocial selling and the 'engineered yes' are compelling. The 'biocontrol of controlling mental processes, emotional reactions and sense perceptions by bioelectrical signals' may not quite be with us, but the means and the motives most certainly are. An enjoyable pseudo-apocryphal, but actually true, experiment in selling was reported in the *Guardian* (7 August 1997). Psychologists from Leicester University operating in a nearby branch of Asda supermarket found that they could 'significantly' influence the sales of particular wines by playing different identifiably ethnic music (French, German, Italian and so on) in the liquor department. The corresponding sales increases in Vin de Table, Liebfraumilch and Chianti were impressive if not entirely surprising. Remember McLean's Nuggets … you heard it here first.

Character Recognition

In a recently published paper entitled 'Automatic extraction of knowledge from student essays,'[6] Maria Vargas Vera and Emanuela Moreale outline how their use of artificial intelligence (AI) techniques enables them to make any recognisable sense out of a student-drafted digital text document. Through the use of a semantic taxonomy, ontological database or conceptual dictionary they explain, for example (using Hyland's taxonomy), how the use of the word 'might' is defined as a hedge as it 'withholds the writer's full commitment to any given statement'. Or using their own taxonomy how the use of 'I accept', 'I am unhappy with' or 'personally' helps to position the author's work in relation to the research of others. What is less clear is how, if at all, this automated analytical process can recognise the unrecognisable original thought. Other recognition systems include HandPunch, Ingersoll Rands 'biometric time and attendance terminals' for fingerprint and iris recognition in a process formerly known as 'clocking-in'. More interesting are Philips' SpeechMagic industrial-grade speech-recognition systems. Speech SDK promises to 'voice

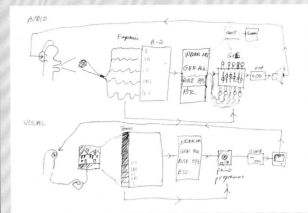

Audio and visual recognition systems schematic, Pete Silver, 1992.

enable any number of products, processes or services', which could certainly make light work of the isolated ardour of the CAD drawing completed in stony-faced silence at the architect's 'studio'. Just tell your local CPU what you want to draw – 'it's like the last project only bigger, without the interesting bits' … now draw. And finally, I have always enjoyed Professor Pete Silver's account of a visit made to Professor Igor Alexander's lab at Imperial College in the early 1990s where he observed the preponderance of the 'toothy grin' researcher, which may or may not have influenced the success of WISARD, the world's first neural pattern-recognition system developed by Alexander and colleagues to determine facial expression. ᴧ

Notes

1. AR Collar and WJ Duncan, *Elementary Matrices and Some Applications to Dynamics and Differential Equations*, Cambridge University Press (Cambridge, UK), 1947.
2. http://www.nasa.gov/centers/dryden/news/NewsReleases/2002/02-18.html.
3. http://www.aer.bris.ac.uk/research/morphing/morph-main.html.
4. http://www.aer.bris.ac.uk/research/morphing/morph-UoB_Research.html.
5. J Krausse and C Lichtenstein, *Your Private Sky: R Buckminster Fuller Discourse*, Lars Müller Publishers (Baden, Switzerland), 2001, pp 253–60.
6. Maria Vargas Vera and Emanuela Moreale, 'Automatic extraction of knowledge from student essays', *International Journal of Knowledge and Learning*, Vol 1, No 4, 2005.

'McLean's Nuggets' is an ongoing technical series inspired by Will McLean and Samantha Hardingham's enthusiasm for back issues of *AD*, as explicitly explored in Hardingham's *AD* issue *The 1970s is Here and Now* (March/April 2005).

Will McLean is joint co-ordinator of Technical Studies (with Pete Silver) in the Department of Architecture at the University of Westminster. He is currently on sabbatical working with Adam Kalkin on his Quik House project in New Jersey, US.

Terrence Donnelly Centre for Cellular and Biomolecular Research

Sean Stanwick describes Behnisch Architects' collaboration with the Canadian firm architectsAlliance on a new laboratory building at the University of Toronto. A 12-storey glass cube with a high-performance skin, it puts its labs on show and decoratively announces its function with colourful glass panels, mimicking the DNA bar code.

It is very likely that few people outside the medical profession will know that Toronto is home to one of the most concentrated clusters of research and medical institutions worldwide. With specialties in bioinformatics and genomics, Toronto's 'Discovery District' and the adjacent Victorian-esque University of Toronto boast the fourth-largest medical research community in North America, while the university's Faculty of Medicine has remained Canada's largest academic institution for 11 years running.

Attracting the best and brightest has always been a mandate for the university, so it is not surprising that an international competition to design a new research facility would attract the most innovative architectural designers as well. Awarded to Germany's Behnisch Architects in a joint venture with Toronto-based architectsAlliance, the technically advanced Terence Donnelly Centre for Cellular and Biomolecular Research (CCBR) is being touted as much for its 'wow factor' as it is for ushering in a new era of scientific and architectural discovery. Of course, the fact that it sits a stone's throw from the new Leslie L Dan Pharmacy Building by Norman Foster certainly adds to the cachet of the project.

Although neither Behnisch nor architectsAlliance had a great depth of laboratory experience, their mutual appreciation of sustainable design and collaborative design philosophy won them the commission in 2001, with construction completed four years later. The $105-million project was funded jointly by the Ontario government, Canada Foundation for Innovation, the university's Infrastructure Investment Fund and through private donor support.

Partner Stefan Behnisch firmly believes in the notion that innovative building science will be the catalyst for new architectural ideas. It is likely the same can be said about a building's influence on architectural awareness, as the CCBR is itself a lesson in Toronto Modernism. Like so many of the city's other modern icons, the 12-storey glass cube revels in its slick aesthetic while politely tipping its hat to its mature counterparts. Set well back from the street, the slender tower stands proud within the newly created urban forecourt. Perched atop a raised granite plinth, the full level grade change from street to front door is traversed by gentle ramps and landscaped terraces. At the seventh floor, the glass facade cuts away to create a deep reveal; in typical Toronto fashion it is a respectful homage to the existing height datum of the historical St George campus.

Decorated with a network of light and colourful glass panels, the skin is both folly and high-performance technology. At first glance, the dance of coloured bars across the east facade appears completely random, yet it actually mimics the DNA bar code. This whimsy, however, belies the science at work here, as the facade is actually a high-

Like so many of the city's other modern icons, the 12-storey glass cube revels in its slick aesthetic and technological innovation while politely tipping its hat to its mature counterparts.

performance double skin. Behnisch has already perfected the system in several projects with a strong sustainability agenda, including his recently completed Genzyme Centre in Cambridge, Massachusetts, already touted as one of the US's most environmentally sustainable office buildings. Factor in shallow, open-concept floor plates, an abundance of natural light and double-height winter gardens that act as lungs for the building, and the CCBR becomes the teacher yet again; only this time it is a lesson in sustainability. In fact, the project has recently been shortlisted for the Lubetkin Prize, awarded for the most outstanding building outside the EU.

The research centre is really about making connections, and often between unlikely bedfellows. Residing somewhere between the historic campus structures and leading-edge

Behnisch Architects and architectsAlliance, Terrence Donnelly Centre for Cellular and Biomolecular Research, Toronto, Canada, 2005
Decorated with a network of light and colourful glass panels, the dance of coloured bars mimics the familiar pattern of the DNA bar code.

To bridge the gaps between historic campus structures and leading-edge technological needs, the architects restored the Romanesque brick facade of the adjacent Rosebrugh Building and incorporated it within the atrium.

The CCBR is a model of sustainability as verdant winter gardens with liriope grass and bamboo trees act as oxygen-rich lungs for the building.

technological needs, it bridges the gaps via textured wooden ramps, or crisp glass and steel stairs. Moving inwards, the white granite and terrazzo forecourt unfolds itself from the street edge to become a towering multistorey atrium, replete with liriope grass and bamboo. Tying into the existing campus circulation routes, this invigorating microclimate actually encourages students to use the building as a short cut to the nearby subway station. Again, playing the good neighbour, the architects restored the Romanesque brick facade of the adjacent Rosebrugh Building and incorporated it within the atrium. Along this meandering promenade, three seminar rooms project through as amoeba-shaped pods, covered with shimmering Italian glass mosaic tiles in shades of russet, charcoal and beige.

But it is on the upper levels that the CCBR literally lights up. Designed to promote the cross-fertilisation of ideas, the top 10 floors are essentially open lofts; a concept also embraced in Will Alsop's recent Queen Mary College Medical Building in London. With a transparent facade that affords spectacular panoramic views both in and out, and few fixed walls to define space, the labs have become a very public spectacle; a far cry from the image of scientists working behind closed doors in hermetically sealed rooms. And knowing that most breakthroughs occur outside the lab, the architects also included a number of off-stage spaces as each floor boasts a café and a communal lounge with hot-wired benches ready for every spontaneous epiphany. △

Based in Toronto, Sean Stanwick is a regular contributor to *AD*, with a particular interest in contemporary architecture and design. He is the co-author of *Wine by Design* (Wiley-Academy, 2005) and *Design City Toronto* (to be published by John Wiley & Sons in March 2007), and has contributed to *Sustaining Architecture in the Anti-Machine Age* (2002), also for Wiley-Academy. He is an instructor with the Royal Architectural Institute of Canada and is currently an associate at Farrow Partnership Architects.

Lab spaces boast a number of off-stage spaces including a communal lounge with hot-wired benches ready for every spontaneous epiphany.

Subscribe Now

As an influential and prestigious architectural publication, *Architectural Design* has an almost unrivalled reputation worldwide. Published bimonthly, it successfully combines the currency and topicality of a newsstand journal with the editorial rigour and design qualities of a book. Consistently at the forefront of cultural thought and design since the 1960s, it has time and again proved provocative and inspirational – inspiring theoretical, creative and technological advances. Prominent in the 1980s and 1990s for the part it played in Postmodernism and then in Deconstruction, in the 2000s *Δ* has leveraged a depth and level of scrutiny not currently offered elsewhere in the design press. Topics pursued question the outcomes of technical innovations as well as the far-reaching social, cultural and environmental challenges that present themselves today in a period of increasing global uncertainty. *Δ*

SUBSCRIPTION RATES 2007
Institutional Rate (Print only or Online only): UK£175/US$315
Institutional Rate (Combined Print and Online): UK£193/US$347
Personal Rate (Print only): UK £110/US$170
Discount Student* Rate (Print only): UK£70/US$110

*Proof of studentship will be required when placing an order. Prices reflect rates for a 2007 subscription and are subject to change without notice.

TO SUBSCRIBE
Phone your credit card order:
+44 (0)1243 843 828

Fax your credit card order to:
+44 (0)1243 770 432

Email your credit card order to:
cs-journals@wiley.co.uk

Δ is available to purchase on both a subscription basis and as individual volumes

Post your credit card or cheque order to:
John Wiley & Sons Ltd.
Journals Administration Department
1 Oldlands Way
Bognor Regis
West Sussex PO22 9SA
UK

Please include your postal delivery address with your order.

All *Δ* volumes are available individually. To place an order please write to:
John Wiley & Sons Ltd
Customer Services
1 Oldlands Way
Bognor Regis
West Sussex PO22 9SA

Please quote the ISBN number of the issue(s) you are ordering.

○ I wish to subscribe to *Δ* Architectural Design at the **Institutional rate of (Print only or Online only** *(delete as applicable)* £175/us$315.

○ I wish to subscribe to *Δ* Architectural Design at the **Institutional rate of (Combined Print and Online) £193/us$347.**

○ I wish to subscribe to *Δ* Architectural Design at the **Personal rate of £110/us$170.**

○ I wish to subscribe to *Δ* Architectural Design at the **Student rate of £70/us$110.**

○ *Δ* Architectural Design is available to individuals on either a calendar year or rolling annual basis; Institutional subscriptions are only available on a calendar year basis. Tick this box if you would like your Personal or Student subscription on a rolling annual basis.

Payment enclosed by Cheque/Money order/Drafts.
Value/Currency £/US$ ☐

○ Please charge £/US$ ☐ to my credit card.
Account number:
☐☐☐☐☐☐☐☐☐☐☐☐☐☐☐☐☐☐

Expiry date:
☐☐☐☐☐☐

Card: Visa/Amex/Mastercard/Eurocard *(delete as applicable)*

Cardholder's signature ☐
Cardholder's name ☐
Address ☐
☐
☐ Post/Zip Code ☐

Recipient's name ☐
Address ☐
☐
☐ Post/Zip Code ☐

I would like to buy the following issues at £22.99 each:

○ *Δ* 185 *Elegance*, Ali Rahim + Hina Jamelle
○ *Δ* 184 *Architextiles*, Mark Garcia
○ *Δ* 183 *Collective Intelligence in Design*, Christopher Hight + Chris Perry
○ *Δ* 182 *Programming Cultures: Art and Architecture in the Age of Software*, Mike Silver
○ *Δ* 181 *The New Europe*, Valentina Croci
○ *Δ* 180 *Techniques and Technologies in Morphogenetic Design*, Michael Hensel, Achim Menges + Michael Weinstock
○ *Δ* 179 *Manmade Modular Megastructures*, Ian Abley + Jonathan Schwinge
○ *Δ* 178 *Sensing the 21st-Century City*, Brian McGrath + Grahame Shane
○ *Δ* 177 *The New Mix*, Sara Caples and Everardo Jefferson
○ *Δ* 176 *Design Through Making*, Bob Sheil
○ *Δ* 175 *Food + The City*, Karen A Franck
○ *Δ* 174 *The 1970s Is Here and Now*, Samantha Hardingham
○ *Δ* 173 *4dspace: Interactive Architecture*, Lucy Bullivant
○ *Δ* 172 *Islam + Architecture*, Sabiha Foster
○ *Δ* 171 *Back To School*, Michael Chadwick
○ *Δ* 170 *The Challenge of Suburbia*, Ilka + Andreas Ruby
○ *Δ* 169 *Emergence*, Michael Hensel, Achim Menges + Michael Weinstock
○ *Δ* 168 *Extreme Sites*, Deborah Gans + Claire Weisz
○ *Δ* 167 *Property Development*, David Sokol
○ *Δ* 166 *Club Culture*, Eleanor Curtis
○ *Δ* 165 *Urban Flashes Asia*, Nicholas Boyarsky + Peter Lang
○ *Δ* 164 *Home Front: New Developments in Housing*, Lucy Bullivant
○ *Δ* 163 *Art + Architecture*, Ivan Margolius
○ *Δ* 162 *Surface Consciousness*, Mark Taylor